Best DIY Projects using Arduino and using Robotic technology

Copyright © Anbazhagan.k
All rights reserved 2019.

Best DIY Projects using Arduino and using Robotic technology

CONTENTS

ACKNOWLEDGMENTS

The writer might want to recognize the diligent work of the article group in assembling this book. He might likewise want to recognize the diligent work of the Raspberry Pi Foundation and the Arduino bunch for assembling items and networks that help to make the Internet Of Things increasingly open to the overall population. Yahoo for the democratization of innovation!

INTRODUCTION

The Internet of Things (IOT) is a perplexing idea comprised of numerous PCs and numerous correspondence ways. Some IOT gadgets are associated with the Internet and some are most certainly not. Some IOT gadgets structure swarms that convey among themselves. Some are intended for a solitary reason, while some are increasingly universally useful PCs. This book is intended to demonstrate to you the IOT from the back to front. By structure IOT gadgets, the per user will comprehend the essential ideas and will almost certainly develop utilizing the rudiments to make his or her very own IOT applications. These included ventures will tell the per user the best way to assemble their very own IOT ventures and to develop the models appeared. The significance of Computer Security in IOT gadgets is additionally talked about and different systems for protecting the IOT from unapproved clients or programmers. The most significant takeaway from this book is in structure the tasks yourself.

1.DC MOTOR CONTROL USING MATLAB AND ARDUINO

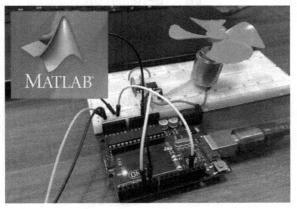

In this instructional exercise, we will tell you the best way to control DC engine utilizing MATLB and Arduino. In the event that you are new with MATLAB, at that point it is prescribe to begin with straightforward LED squint program with MATLAB.

Creating MATLAB Graphical User Interface for controlling DC Motor

Subsequent to completing arrangement with Arduino for MATLAB, we need to fabricate GUI (Graphical User Interface) to control DC engine. To dispatch the GUI, type the beneath direction in the order window

---

guide

A popup window will open, at that point select new clear GUI as appeared in beneath picture,

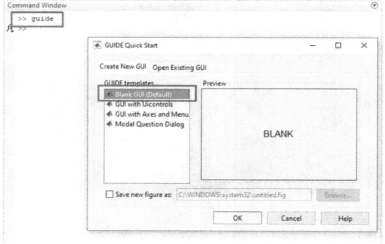

Presently pick three pushbuttons for Clockwise revolution, Anti-clockwise turn and STOP, as demonstrated as follows,

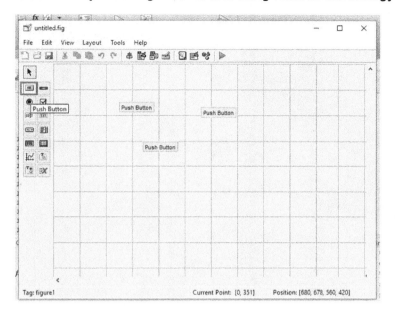

To resize or to change the state of the catch, simply click on it and most likely you will drag the sides of the catch. By double tapping on pushbutton you can change the shading, string and tag of that specific catch. We have redone three catches as appeared in beneath picture.

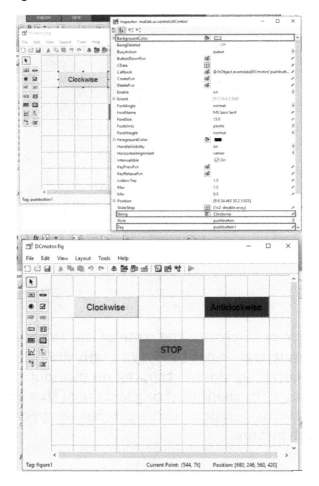

You can redo the catches according to your decision. Presently when you spare this, a code is produced in the Editor window of MATLAB. To code your Arduino for playing out any assignment identified with your venture, you generally need to alter this created code. So underneath we have altered the MATLAB code.

MATLAB Code for controlling DC Motor with Arduino

Complete MATLAB code, subsequent to altering it for DC engine control, is given toward the part of the bargain. Further we are including the GUI record (.fig) and code file(.m) here for download, utilizing which you can redo the catches according to your necessity. The following are a few changes we accomplished for turning the DC Motor clockwise, anticlockwise and quit utilizing three push catches.

Reorder the beneath code on line no. 74 to ensure that the Arduino is chatting with MATLAB each time you run the m-document.

```
clear all;

global a;

a = arduino();
```

```
64
65    % --- Outputs from this function are returned to the command line.
66    ⊟function varargout = DCmotor_OutputFcn(hObject, eventdata, handles)
67    ⊟% varargout   cell array for returning output args (see VARARGOUT);
68    % hObject     handle to figure
69    % eventdata   reserved - to be defined in a future version of MATLAB
70    % handles     structure with handles and user data (see GUIDATA)
71
72    % Get default command line output from handles structure
73 -  varargout{1} = handles.output;
74 -  clear all;
75 -  global a;
76 -  a = arduino();
77
```

When you look down, you will note three capacities for each Button in the GUI. Presently compose the code in each capacity as per task you want to perform on snap.

In Clockwise catch's capacity, reorder the beneath code just before the closure props of the capacity to pivot the engine clockwise way. Here we are giving HIGH at stick 6 and LOW at stick 5 to pivot the engine clockwise way.

global a;

writeDigitalPin(a, 'D5', 0);

writeDigitalPin(a, 'D6', 1);

pause(0.5);

```
90      % --- Executes on button press in pushbutton2.
91    □ function anticlockwise_Callback(hObject, eventdata, handles)
92    □ % hObject      handle to pushbutton2 (see GCBO)
93      % eventdata   reserved - to be defined in a future version of MATLAB
94    ├ % handles     structure with handles and user data (see GUIDATA)
95 -    global a;
96 -    writeDigitalPin(a, 'D5', 1);
97 -    writeDigitalPin(a, 'D6', 0);
98 -   └ pause(0.5);
```

Presently in Anti-clockwise catch's capacity, glue the underneath code toward the part of the bargain to pivot the engine in hostile to clockwise course. Here we are giving HIGH at stick 5 and LOW at stick 6 to turn the engine in Anti-clockwise course.

global a;

writeDigitalPin(a, 'D5', 0);

writeDigitalPin(a, 'D6', 0);

pause(0.5);

At long last in STOP catch's capacity, glue the beneath code toward the end, to stop the turn of engine. Here we are giving LOW at both stick 5 and 6 to stop the engine.

global a;

```
writeDigitalPin(a, 'D5', 0);

writeDigitalPin(a, 'D6', 0);

pause(0.5);
```

```
100
101    % --- Executes on button press in pushbutton3.
102    function stop_Callback(hObject, eventdata, handles)
103    % hObject    handle to pushbutton3 (see GCBO)
104    % eventdata  reserved - to be defined in a future version of MATLAB
105    % handles    structure with handles and user data (see GUIDATA)
106 -  global a;
107 -  writeDigitalPin(a, 'D5', 0);
108 -  writeDigitalPin(a, 'D6', 0);
109 -  pause(0.5);
110
```

Material Required

1. Arduino UNO
2. MATLAB introduced Laptop (Preference: R2016a or above renditions)
3. L293D- motor driver
4. DC Motor

Circuit Diagram

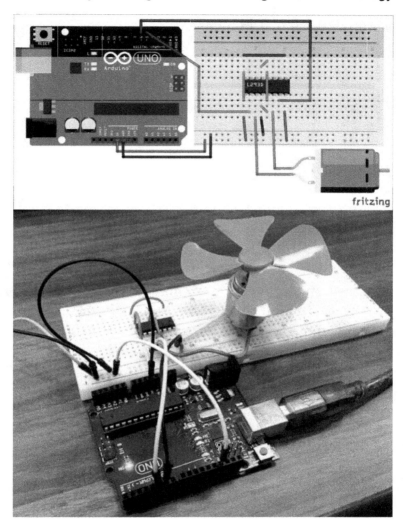

Controlling DC Motor with MATLAB

After arrangement the equipment as indicated by circuit outline, simply click on the run catch to run

the altered code in .m record

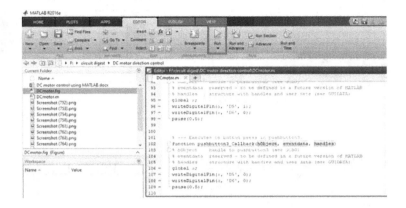

MATLAB may take few moments to react, don't tap on any GUI catch until MATLAB shows BUSY sign, which you can see at the left base corner of the screen as demonstrated as follows,

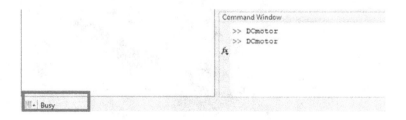

When everything is prepared, click on clockwise or anticlockwise catch to pivot the engine. When you press Clockwise catch current move through Pin 6 to Pin 5 and engine will pivot clockwise way while in anticlockwise current moves through Pin 5 to Pin 6

and engine will turn clockwise way will pivot clockwise way. To stop the pivot of DC engine press STOP catch. Same strategy can be utilized to control the servo Motor utilizing MATLAB, we simply need to an alter the code as needs be.

Code

```
function varargout = DCmotor(varargin)
gui_Singleton = 1;
gui_State = struct('gui_Name',    mfilename, ...
        'gui_Singleton', gui_Singleton, ...
        'gui_OpeningFcn', @DCmotor_OpeningFcn, ...
        'gui_OutputFcn', @DCmotor_OutputFcn, ...
        'gui_LayoutFcn', [], ...
        'gui_Callback',  []);
if nargin && ischar(varargin{1})
   gui_State.gui_Callback = str2func(varargin{1});
end
if nargout
    [varargout{1:nargout}] = gui_mainfcn(gui_State, varargin{:});
else
   gui_mainfcn(gui_State, varargin{:});
end
function DCmotor_OpeningFcn(hObject, eventdata, handles, varargin)
guidata(hObject, handles);
function varargout = DCmotor_OutputFcn(hObject, eventdata, handles)
```

```
varargout{1} = handles.output;
clear all;
global a;
a = arduino();
function  clockwise_Callback(hObject,  eventdata,
handles)
global a;
writeDigitalPin(a, 'D5', 0);
writeDigitalPin(a, 'D6', 1);
pause(0.5);
function  anticlockwise_Callback(hObject,  event-
data, handles)
global a;
writeDigitalPin(a, 'D5', 1);
writeDigitalPin(a, 'D6', 0);
pause(0.5);
function stop_Callback(hObject, eventdata, handles)
global a;
writeDigitalPin(a, 'D5', 0);
writeDigitalPin(a, 'D6', 0);
pause(0.5);
```

2.SMART PHONE CONTROLLED ARDUINO MOOD LIGHT WITH ALARM

I as of late bought the Neo Pixel LED strip and was very dazzled by the manner in which it works. The minor LED's have an inbuilt driver IC which encourages us to control each LED separately and can create a vast range of hues. Being a conspicuous individual who is fixated on hues I truly adored viewing these minor LED's changing hues so I chose to fabricate something all alone and leave it shading my room during evening times.

I needed these LED's to change hues as well as have rationale thinking behind it. That is the point at which I ran over the article by Mr. Stephen Westland who is an educator of Color Science and Technology at University of Leeds. He guarantees that when people are presented to shaded lights they react, both physiologically and mentally dependent on the shading. This idea isn't new and has been broadly polished for the sake of Chromotherapy and the gadget used to do this is known as a Mood Lamp.

So I at last settled to dive profound into chromotherapy and assemble a Mood Lamp which could change hues dependent on the time and can likewise be controlled structure the cell phone. Aside from that I additionally added a LDR to turn it off naturally during day time and furthermore a choice to set a wake up caution which will wake you up with a splendid orange shading (daylight) and another alert that places the LED's in rest mode with gentle purple (night sky) shading to rest you into rest. Sounds fascinating right? So how about we get building.

Chromotherapy – Mood Lamp

Be that as it may, there are bunches of supposed DIY disposition lights out there which just arbitrarily change shading with no reason behind it. After a touch of looking through I found that a mind-set light ought to have at least certain lumens brilliance and ought to likewise change hues bit by bit with differing force. Each shading differently affects both mental and physical level. I have arranged the effect against each shading in the underneath table.

Colour	Physiological impact	Physical impact
Red	Gives more Energy, Boosts Sexual Desires	Kidney, Backbone, sense of smell
Yellow	Improves Digestion, Kills Depression	Stomach, Liver, Intestine
Blue	Lowers Blood Pressure, Calm Down People	Migraine headache, throat, ears and mouth
Green	Stimulates Growth and strengthens muscle	Bones, tissues, immune system
Purple	Sleep Inducer Emotional and Mental Balance Decreases Sexual desires	Nervous system, eyes
Orange	Stimulates creativity	Breathing, Brest feeding
Pink	Purifies Blood	Blood, arteries, veins

So dependent on this information I have structured the disposition Lamp to change its hues dependent on what time it is. Obviously I have included some close to home flavor, so don't hesitate to alter the program likewise.

Materials Required

Enough science we should work with gadgets, so how about we assemble the required segments.

- 12V Power supply
- Arduino
- Neo Pixel LEDs
- HC-05 Bluetooth Module
- DS3231 RTC module
- 100K resistor
- LDR

Circuit Diagram

The total circuit chart for this Bluetooth Controlled Arduino Mood Lamp Project is given underneath.

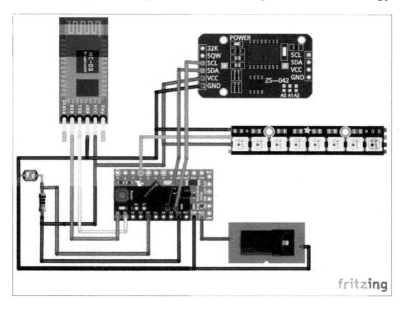

As should be obvious, we have utilized modules and henceforth the associations are pretty basically. For monitoring the present time we have utilized the DS3231 Real Time Clock (RTC) module. This module works with the assistance of I2C correspondence and can be fueled straightforwardly with 5V stick of the Arduino. The SDA and SCL pins are associated with the I2C pins A4 and A5 individually.

Next we have utilized the HC-05 Bluetooth module. Through this Bluetooth association we can set the required shading on the LED and furthermore set a rest time and wake up time for the LED. The Bluetooth module is fueled with the 5V stick also and the Tx and Rx pins are associated with Arduino through pins 11 and 10 separately.

It is silly to gleam the LEDs when the room is brilliant, henceforth we have utilized a LDR to identify splendor in the room and on the off chance that it is splendid the LEDs mood killer consequently and betrays just when the room is dim is sufficient. We have framed a potential divider coordinate with one resistor being simply the LDR and the other a 100K resistor and interface it to stick A0 of Arduino, along these lines a the obstruction of LDR fluctuates dependent on light the voltage perused by the Arduino will likewise change. Get familiar with interfacing LDR with Arduino here.

At long last the neo pixel is associated with stick 6 of Arduino which is a PWM stick and is again controlled by the 5V stick (vcc) of the Arduino. I have utilized an Arduino Pro-scaled down for my venture since it is littler and would be helpful while pressing it inside a walled in area. You can utilize any leading body of your decision. The total set-up is fueled by a 12V connector which is associated with the RAW stick of the Arduino. The on board voltage controller on Arduino changes over this 12V to 5V which is then used to supply 5V to power every one of the modules through the vcc stick.

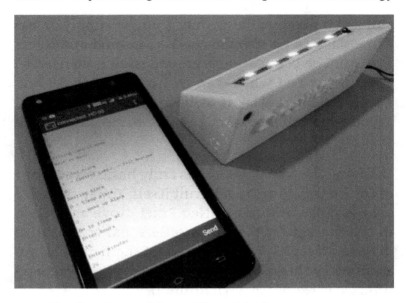

Neo Pixel LEDs and How They Work

The essential and cool segment of this venture is the neo Pixel LED. The thought for the Neo pixel LEDs were initially by the Adafruit ventures in which they utilize a LED driver IC WS2812 inside a RBG LED. This driver IC can get a control signal from a controller like Arduino and dependent on the control signal it can control the power of the RBG shading therefore helping us to accomplish the required shading.

You can associate the similar number of as of these LED in arrangement and the cool element is that every one of these LED can be tended to exclusively meaning each LED can be made to gleam in various hues by tweaking the control signal as needs be. So recall that not at all like a typical LED you can control a neo pixel utilizing only a power supply, it has three stick to be specific the Vcc, ground and information. The Vcc as well as ground stick is utilized to control the Led which can go from 3.3V to 5V and the information stick is utilized to send the control signal which choose what Led should gleam in which shading.

Utilizing the Neo pixel LED is truly basic on account of the library given by Adafruit itself. Today there are a wide range of kinds of Neo Pixel drove accessible in the market from various sellers and they utilize diverse driver IC. Yet, every one of them can be constrained by this Adafruit library. We have beforehand interfaced NeoPixel with Arduino.

Programming Arduino for Mood Light

The total program for this Neo-pixel disposition light with Arduino undertaking is given toward the part of the arrangement, which can be utilized accordingly after you have included the required libraries. In this segment I will talk about couple of significant bits from the code which could enable you to change the venture as required. The program is very enormous around 300 lines so in case you feel testy attempting to comprehend anything doesn't hesitate to post your inquiries on the discussions and as constantly complete Arduino program can be found toward the part of the arrangement.

As consistently we start the program by including the

required libraries for the task for this situation the accompanying libraries are required.

```
#include <SoftwareSerial.h> //Bluetooth module
works with software serial

#include <Adafruit_NeoPixel.h> //Library for Neo
Pixel (Download from Link in article)

#include <DS3231.h> //Library for RTC module
(Download from Link in article)

#include <EEPROM.h> //Library for EEPROM (Pre-
Loaded into Arduino)
```

The Bluetooth module works however sequential correspondence; I don't lean toward utilizing the equipment sequential stick (0 and 1) for that since I will utilize the sequential screen to troubleshoot the program, so we incorporate the product sequential library into our program. This library will be available in your IDE as a matter of course.

Next we utilize the Adafruit Neo Pixel library from Adafruit that we talked about in past heading. You can download the Adafruit Neo pixel library utilizing the connection, which will download the ZIP document from the GitHub. At that point you can utilize the sketch - > Include Library - > Add .ZIP library alternative to include this ZIP document into your Arduino IDE.

Additionally you can likewise download the DS3231 library for the RTC module and include it a similar way. At long last we have EEPROM library which are now pre-stacked into the Arduino library. We simply need to add the library to store the wake up alert and rest caution time in EEPROM with the goal that when the Arduino re-boots after a power disappointment it recalls when to rest and when to wake up.

The Neo Pixel LEDs can deliver a wide scope of hues, yet we are not inspired by every one of the hues for our state of mind light aside from 8 of them which are Red, Orange, Yellow, Green, Cyan, Blue, Purple and Pink. To get every one of these hues we need to pass its particular estimation. So we characterize the estimation of each shading utilizing the macros as demonstrated as follows.

```
#define Red 1

#define Orange 20

#define Yellow 30

#define Green 70

#define Cyan 100
```

```
#define Blue 130

#define Purple 200

#define Pink 240
```

Next we need to announce to which pins we have associated the neo Pixel and what number of LEDs are available on the Neo Pixel strip. For my situation I have associated the Neo pixel to stick 6 as appeared in the circuit graph above and I have an aggregate of 5 LEDs on my strip so my code resembles

```
Adafruit_NeoPixel strip = Adafruit_NeoPixel(5, 6,
NEO_GRB + NEO_KHZ800); //5 LEDs on PIN-6
```

There are a huge deal of worldwide factors proclaimed in the program in the following line, what you may be intrigued to play around is with the cluster assertions. There are two exhibits in particular the morning_rainbow and evening_rainbow each comprising of 4 hues. I have chosen Red, Orange, Green and Pink to be the morning hues and Yellow, Cyan, Blue and Purple to be the night hues dependent on the chromo treatment table that we talked about above you can transform it as you wish

```
//array declarations
```

```
char current_rainbow[8] = {}; //the main array

char morning_rainbow[4] = {Red, Orange, Green,
Pink}; //colours to show during day time

char evening_rainbow[4] = {Yellow, Cyan, Blue,
Purple}; //colours to show during night time

char all_rainbow[8] = {Red, Orange, Yellow, Green,
Cyan, Blue, Purple, Pink}; //colours that can be con-
trolled thorugh Bluetooth
```

Inside the void arrangement work we initialise the Bluetooth module and Serial screen at 9600 baud rate. The Bluetooth is utilized to speak with our telephone and the sequential screen is utilized for troubleshooting. Basically dispatch the sequential screen and you can screen all the crucial factors in the program. Aside from that we additionally read the EEPROM esteems if the client has set them already and store them in the particular factors

```
void setup(){//Execute once during the launch of
program

    Initialize_RTC();

    Bluetooth.begin(9600);
```

```
Serial.begin (9600); //for debugging

strip.begin();

strip.show(); // Initialize all pixels to 'off'

Bluetooth.println("Mood Lamp Alarm -Hello");

Serial.println("Mood Lamp Alarm -Hello");

//If anything was stored previously in EEPROM
copy it to the alarm variables

   sleep_alarm_hour = EEPROM.read(0);

   sleep_alarm_minute = EEPROM.read(1);

   wake_alarm_hour = EEPROM.read(2);

   wake_alarm_minute = EEPROM.read(3);

}
```

Inside the fundamental circle, we start the program by perusing the incentive from the LDR, if the room is brilliant the program darken every one of the LEDs in this manner turning it off and after that trusts that the room will get splendid once more. The capacity Interactive_BT is likewise checked when the room is splendid with the goal that the client can in any case power the lights to divert on from the cell phone. Here I have select 800 as the edge esteem yet in case you need to light to work even in brilliant sunshine you can basically build the estimation of 800. At that point range is structure 0-1024.

```
while (lightvalue>800) //IF the room is very brigt
(you can increase this values to make it glow even
duringf day)

    {

        for (int i=0; i<=5; i++) //turn of all LED

        {

            strip.setBrightness(0); //by setting bright-
ness to zero

            strip.show();

        }

    lightvalue = analogRead(A0); //kepp checking if
    the room is getting darker

    Serial.print("Too bright to glow: ");

    Serial.println(lightvalue); //for debugging
```

```
Interactive_BT(); //Also check if the user is try-
ing to access through bluetooth

delay(100);

}
```

The interactive_BT is the capacity inside which the client can set the alert or control the Lamp from his telephone. The code inside this capacity is simple through remark area, so I am not going line by line. The claim to fame of the program is that it can utilize any Bluetooth application from android application store or Iphone store and still can collaborate with it.

Next we read the present time and update the time object "t". From that we split the hour and moment worth utilizing the t.hour and t.min and store it in the variable current_time_hour and current_time_minute individually.

```
t = rtc.getTime(); //get the current time

current_time_hour = t.hour; //get hour value

current_time_minute = t.min; //get minute value
```

In this program I am changing the shade of the Neo pixel for at regular intervals, so the following section for code will be execute just once in like clock-work. Inside this section we increment the estima-tion of check and call the capacity called glow_rain-bow. This capacity gleams the drove dependent on the hues put away in the current_rainbow exhibit. So before calling this gleam rainbow we need to stack current rainbow utilizing a lot of hues from either morning_rainbow or evening_rainbow dependent on the time as demonstrated as follows.

```
if (sleeping == false) //If we are not sleeping

    glow_rainbow(colour_count);    //dsplay the
colours

    if (sleeping == true) //if we are sleeping

    night_lamp(); //display the night lamp effect

    if (t.hour>=17) //During evening time

    {

    for (int i=0; i<=3; i++)

    { current_rainbow[i] = evening_rainbow[i]; de-
lay(100);} //copy evening raninbow into cur-
rent_rainbow
```

```
}

else //During Morning

{

  for (int i=0; i<=3; i++)

  { current_rainbow[i] = morning_rainbow[i]; de-
lay(100);} //copy  mornign rainboe into current
rainbow

}
```

Inside the glow_rainbow work we utilize two for circles one to diminish the LED and other to expand
the brilliance of the LED dependent on the required
shading. This required shading is chosen from the
exhibit current_rainboe[count] where check chooses
the present shading structure the cluster. There are
absolutely 5 LED in my strip so I have utilized variable I upto 5, the estimation of j can be fiddled around
between 0-255 as per how much ever brilliance you
need to lessen

```
void glow_rainbow(int count)

{
```

```
    for (int j=150; j>=10; j--) //decrease the bright-
ness to create dim effect

    {

        for (int i=0; i<=5; i++) //do it for all 5 leds

        {

            strip.setBrightness(j);

            strip.show();

        }

        1    delay(2);

    }

    for (int j=0; j<=255; j++) //increase the brightness

    {

        for (int i=0; i<=5; i++) //do it for all 5 leds

        {

            strip.setPixelColor(i,Wheel(current_rain-
bow[count]));//select the colour based on count
value
```

```
        strip.setBrightness(j);

        strip.show();

    }

        delay(10);

}

}
```

The capacity wheel is legitimately taken from the Adafruit model program. It takes in an incentive since 0 to 255 and produces a shading dependent on the worth. This worth is the thing that we characterized at first in our program utilizing the #define macros. The capacity is demonstrated as follows.

```
// Input a value 0 to 255 to get a color value.

// The colours are a transition r - g - b - back to r.

uint32_t Wheel(byte WheelPos) {

WheelPos = 255 - WheelPos;

if(WheelPos < 85) {
```

```
    return strip.Color( (255 - WheelPos * 3), 0,
(WheelPos * 3) );

    }

    if(WheelPos < 170) {

      WheelPos -= 85;

      return strip.Color(0, (WheelPos * 3) , (255 -
WheelPos * 3) );

    }

    WheelPos -= 170;

    return strip.Color((WheelPos * 3), (255 - Wheel-
Pos) * 3, 0);

    }
```

This line strip.Color(x,y,z) is a significant line which chooses the shade of the LED. The factors x,y and z each take an incentive from 0-255 and dependent on the worth it chooses the measure of Red, Green and Blue light the LED ought to discharge. So x,y advertisement z legitimately controls the Red, Green as well as Blue light force of the LED pixels.

Controlling and Setting Alarm through Smart Phone

When you have made the association according to the circuit outline and have transferred the code given beneath you can test the circuit. I would likewise prescribe opening the sequential screen to check how the equipment is reacting to the program. When you are completed you can open your Bluetooth application on the cell phone.

I am utilizing the Bluetooth terminal application from Play Store yet you can utilize any Bluetooth application which encourages you to peruse and compose information through Bluetooth association. Ensure you have matched the Bluetooth module with your telephone utilizing the secret key "1234" preceding propelling the application. When the application is propelled interface with your Bluetooth gadget which ought to be typical named as "HC-05".

To start interchanges simply send an irregular variable from the telephone, for this situation I have sent 'g'. This will start Interactive Bluetooth correspondence mode in the program and you will get the accompanying screen.

Anbazhagan k

From here essentially adhere to the on screen guidance to set caution or for controlling the light for your required shading by just send numbers. For instance I have set the morning alert here.

Additionally you can likewise set the night caution and can control the Lamp by sending the number for required shading as demonstrated as follows.

connected: HC-05

```
1 -> Wake up Alarm
1
Wake me at:
Enter hours
06
Enter minutes
30
Wake up alarm set at: 6 : 30
Back to main
x
0-> Set Alarm
1 -> Control Lamp
x -> Exit Anytime
1
Select the colour you like
0-> Red
1-> Orange
2-> Yellow
3-> Green
4-> Cyan
5-> Blue
6-> Purple
7-> Pink
7
2
```

Send

3D Printing the Enclosure for Arduino Mood Light

As I said I made this task to be left working in my office or in my family room so it requires a decent nook for lodging all the hardware. Likewise it harms our eyes to take a gander at the pixel straightforwardly when they shine. So I choose to 3D print my fenced in area utilizing my Tevo tarantula printer and consequently proceeded to structure my walled in areas.

The total plan records are accessible for download from thingiverse. You can likewise print your very own in case you have 3D printer or just can utilize wood or acrylic to fabricate a walled in area of our own. My print setting is appear in the picture underneath.

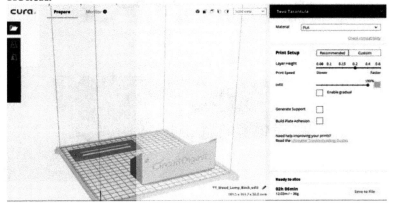

As a result of printing you can push the LDR into the little opening gave and the LED strip can be slide into the top case. As a result of collecting, my equipment looked something like this as demonstrated as follows.

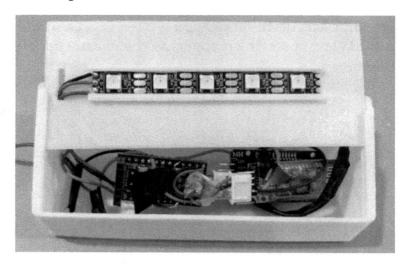

All that is left to do is control the set-up utilizing a 12V connector and set the alert utilizing the Bluetooth choice as talked about above and leave in lighting up your room. Expectation you loved the undertaking and appreciated structure it. In case you have confronted any issue in the manufacture procedure you can post it in the remark segment underneath or utilize the discussions for snappy assistance.

Code

```
/*
* Mood light using Arduino
* Interactive Bluetooth Programming using Terminal
* Alarm function for wake up and sleep.

*/
```

```
/*PIN CONNECTIONS
* Bluetooth (HC-05)
* #Tx -> 11
* Rx -> 10
* #DS3231 (RTC)
* SDA -> A4
* SCL -> A5
* #Neo Pixel
* Data -> pin 6
*/
```

#include <SoftwareSerial.h> //Bluetooth module works with software serial

#include <Adafruit_NeoPixel.h> //Library for Neo Pixel (Download from Link in article)

#include <DS3231.h> //Library for RTC module (Download from Link in article)

#include <SPI.h> //Library for SPI communication (Pre-Loaded into Arduino)

#include <EEPROM.h> //Library for EEPROM (Pre-Loaded into Arduino)

//Define the value of colours

#define Red 1

#define Orange 20

#define Yellow 30

#define Green 70

#define Cyan 100

#define Blue 130

#define Purple 200

#define Pink 240

Adafruit_NeoPixel strip = Adafruit_NeoPixel(5, 6,

```
NEO_GRB + NEO_KHZ800); //5 LEDs on PIN-6
DS3231 rtc(SDA, SCL); //object for RTC module
Time t; //element t
SoftwareSerial Bluetooth(11, 10); // TX, RX

//GLOBAL variables
char incoming; //to store value form Bluetooth
int lightvalue=0; //LDR output vale
int colour_count = 0; //to increment array
//variable to store hour and minute values
int wake_alarm_hour;
int sleep_alarm_hour;
int wake_alarm_minute;
int sleep_alarm_minute;
int current_time_hour;
int current_time_minute;
//flag variables
boolean settings = false;
boolean sleeping = false;
//array declarations
char current_rainbow[8] = {}; //the main array
char morning_rainbow[4] = {Red, Orange, Green,
Pink}; //colours to show during day time
char evening_rainbow[4] = {Yellow, Cyan, Blue, Pur-
ple}; //colours to show during night time
char all_rainbow[8] = {Red, Orange, Yellow, Green,
Cyan, Blue, Purple, Pink}; //colours that can be con-
trolled thorugh bluetooth
void wait_for_reply() //Function to wait for user to
enter value for BT
```

```
{
Bluetooth.flush(); while (!Bluetooth.available());
}
void Initialize_RTC()
{
rtc.begin();  // Initialize the rtc object
//#### The following lines can be uncommented to
set the date and time for the first time###
//rtc.setDOW(TUESDAY);     // Set Day-of-Week to
SUNDAY
//rtc.setTime(13, 01, 00);  // Set the time to 12:00:00
(24hr format)
//rtc.setDate(9, 25, 2018);  // Set the date to January
1st, 2014
}
    int get_hour() //get the hour value for setting alarm
{
char UD; char LD; //upper digit and lower digit
Bluetooth.println("Enter hours");
wait_for_reply(); //wait for user to enter something
 UD = Bluetooth.read(); delay (100); //Read the first
digit
wait_for_reply(); //wait for user to enter something
LD = Bluetooth.read(); //Read the lower digit
 UD= int(UD)-48; LD= int(LD)-48; //convert the char
to int by subtracting 48 from it
  return (UD*10)+ LD; // Comine the uper digit and
lowe digit to form the number which is hours
}
```

```
int get_minute() //get the minute value for setting
alarm
{
char UD; char LD; //upper digit and lower digit
Bluetooth.println("Enter minutes");
wait_for_reply();//wait for user to enter something
 UD = Bluetooth.read(); delay (100); //Read the first
digit
wait_for_reply();//wait for user to enter something
LD = Bluetooth.read(); //Read the first digit
 UD= int(UD)-48; LD= int(LD)-48; //convert the char
to int by subtracting 48 from it
 return (UD*10)+ LD; // Comine the uper digit and
lowe digit to form the number which is hours
}




void setup(){//Execute once during the launch of
program
 Initialize_RTC();
 Bluetooth.begin(9600);
 Serial.begin (9600); //for debugging


  strip.begin();
 strip.show(); // Initialize all pixels to 'off'
```

```
  Bluetooth.println("Mood Lamp Alarm -Hello");
  Serial.println("Mood Lamp Alarm -Hello");
//If anything was stored previously in EEPROM copy
it to the alarm variables
  sleep_alarm_hour = EEPROM.read(0);
  sleep_alarm_minute = EEPROM.read(1);
  wake_alarm_hour = EEPROM.read(2);
  wake_alarm_minute = EEPROM.read(3);
}
void loop(){
  lightvalue = analogRead(A0); //Read the value form
LDR


  while (lightvalue>800) //IF the room is very brigt
(you can increase this values to make it glow even
duringf day)
  {
    for (int i=0; i<=5; i++) //turn of all LED
    {
      strip.setBrightness(0); //by setting brightness to
zero
      strip.show();
    }
  lightvalue = analogRead(A0); //kepp checking if the
room is getting darker
  Serial.print("Too bright to glow: ");
  Serial.println(lightvalue); //for debugging
  Interactive_BT(); //Also check if the user is trying to
access through bluetooth
```

```
  delay(100);
}
```

```
  settings=true; //if setting is true it means we have
are ready to get into bluetooth control
  Interactive_BT(); //Also check if the user is trying to
access through bluetooth
```

```
  t = rtc.getTime(); //get the current time
current_time_hour = t.hour; //get hour value
current_time_minute = t.min; //get minute value
    if(t.sec%5 == 0) //For every 5 seconds
{
  colour_count++; //change the colour
  if(colour_count>=4) //if we exceed array count
  colour_count = 0; //initialise the count
    while(t.sec%5==0) //wait till the 5th secound is
over
  t = rtc.getTime(); //update t.sec
    //For Debugging
    Serial.print ("Glowing clour: ");Serial.println(col-
our_count);
    Serial.print("At time: "); Serial.print(t.hour); Ser-
ial.print (" : "); Serial.println (t.min);
        Serial.print("Enviroment Brightness: "); Ser-
```

```
ial.println(lightvalue);
        Serial.print("Wake up at :"); Serial.print(
wake_alarm_hour); Serial.print (" : "); Serial.println
(wake_alarm_minute);
        Serial.print("Sleep at :"); Serial.print(
sleep_alarm_hour); Serial.print (" : "); Serial.println
(sleep_alarm_minute);
    Serial.print ("Is Lamp sleeping? : "); Serial.println
(sleeping);
    Serial.println("        ******        ");
    //End of debugging lines
    if(sleeping == false) //If we are not sleeping
    glow_rainbow(colour_count); //dsplay the colours
    if(sleeping == true) //if we are sleeping
    night_lamp(); //display the night lamp effect
    if(t.hour>=17) //During evening time
{
  for (int i=0; i<=3; i++)
        { current_rainbow[i] = evening_rainbow[i];
delay(100);} //copy evening raninbow into cur-
rent_rainbow
}
else //During Morning
{
  for (int i=0; i<=3; i++)
      { current_rainbow[i] = morning_rainbow[i]; de-
lay(100);} //copy mornign rainboe into current rain-
bow
}
```

```
}
```

if(t.hour == sleep_alarm_hour && t.min == sleep_alarm_minute) //If the sleep time is meat
{ sleeping = true; Serial.println("Lamp getting into Sleep Mode");}//get into sleeping mode

if(t.hour == wake_alarm_hour && t.min == wake_alarm_minute)// If wake up time is meat
{ sleeping = false; Serial.println("Lamp is up and ready"); }// get out of sleeping mode.
}
void Interactive_BT() //using this funciton the user cna control LED colour and set alarm time.
{

if(Bluetooth.available() > 0 && settings == true) { // if the user has sent something
incoming = Bluetooth.read(); //read and clear the stack
Bluetooth.println("0-> Set Alarm "); Bluetooth.println("1 -> Control Lamp"); Bluetooth.println("x -> Exit Anytime"); //Display the options
wait_for_reply();
incoming = Bluetooth.read(); //read what the user has sent
//Based on user request
if(incoming == '0') //if user sent 0

```
{
        Bluetooth.println("Setting    Alarm");
Bluetooth.println("0->    Sleep    alarm");    Blue-
tooth.println("1 -> Wake up Alarm"); //give alarm op-
tions
wait_for_reply();
incoming = Bluetooth.read();


    if(incoming == '0')
    {
            Bluetooth.println("Go to sleep at:");
sleep_alarm_hour = get_hour(); sleep_alarm_minute
= get_minute();
        Bluetooth.print("Sleep alarm set at: "); Blue-
tooth.print(sleep_alarm_hour); Bluetooth.print(":");
Bluetooth.println(sleep_alarm_minute);
        EEPROM.write(0, sleep_alarm_hour); EEPROM.
write(1, sleep_alarm_minute);
    }


    if(incoming == '1')
    {
            Bluetooth.println("Wake me at:");
wake_alarm_hour = get_hour(); wake_alarm_minute
= get_minute();
        Bluetooth.print("Wake up alarm set at: "); Blue-
tooth.print(wake_alarm_hour); Bluetooth.print(" :
"); Bluetooth.println(wake_alarm_minute);
        EEPROM.write(2, wake_alarm_hour); EEPROM.
```

```
write(3, wake_alarm_minute);
    }
    incoming = 'x';
}
   if (incoming == '1')
   {
   Bluetooth.println("Select the colour you like");
   Bluetooth.println("0-> Red"); Bluetooth.println("1-
> Orange"); Bluetooth.println("2-> Yellow"); Blue-
tooth.println("3->  Green");  Bluetooth.println("4->
Cyan");
              Bluetooth.println("5->  Blue");  Blue-
tooth.println("6->  Purple");  Bluetooth.println("7->
Pink");
     do{
   wait_for_reply();
   incoming = Bluetooth.read();
     memcpy(current_rainbow, all_rainbow, 8);


     glow_rainbow(incoming-48);
   Serial.println(incoming-48);
   }while (incoming!='x');
     Bluetooth.println("Exiting control mode");
}
   if (incoming == 'x') //exit from Bluetooth mode
   {
   Bluetooth.flush();
   incoming = Bluetooth.read();
   incoming = 0;
```

```
    settings= false;
    Bluetooth.println("Back to main");
  }
  }
}


// Input a value 0 to 255 to get a color value.
// The colours are a transition r - g - b - back to r.
uint32_t Wheel(byte WheelPos) {
 WheelPos = 255 - WheelPos;
 if(WheelPos < 85) {
   return strip.Color( (255 - WheelPos * 3), 0, (Wheel-
Pos * 3) );
 }
 if(WheelPos < 170) {
  WheelPos -= 85;
   return strip.Color(0, (WheelPos * 3) , (255 - Wheel-
Pos * 3) );
 }
 WheelPos -= 170;
 return strip.Color((WheelPos * 3), (255 - WheelPos) *
3, 0);
}


void glow_rainbow(int count)
{
  for (int j=150; j>=10; j--) //decrease the brightness to
create dim effect
  {
   for (int i=0; i<=5; i++) //do it for all 5 leds
```

```
    {
      strip.setBrightness(j);
      strip.show();
    }
      delay(2);
    }



    for (int j=0; j<=255; j++) //increase the brightness
    {
      for (int i=0; i<=5; i++) //do it for all 5 leds
      {
          strip.setPixelColor(i,Wheel(current_rainbow[
    count]));//select the colour based on count value
        strip.setBrightness(j);
        strip.show();
      }
          delay(10);
    }
    }
    void night_lamp()
    {
    for (int j=240; j<=254; j++) //decrease the brightness
    to create dim effect
    {
     for (int i=0; i<=5; i++)//do it for all 5 leds
      {
        strip.setPixelColor(i, 255-j, 0, 255-j);
        strip.show();
```

```
    }
  delay(300);
}
for (int j=254; j>=240; j--)//decrease the brightness to
create dim effect
{
{
  for (int i=0; i<=5; i++)//do it for all 5 leds
    {
      strip.setPixelColor(i, 255-j, 0, 255-j);
      strip.show();
    }
  delay(300);
}
}
}
```

3.INTERFACING NRF24L01 WITH ARDUINO: CONTROLLING SERVO MOTOR

While IoT, Industry 4.0, Machine to Machine correspondence and so on are getting progressively mainstream the requirement for remote correspondence has turned out to be occupant, with more machines/gadgets to talk with each other on the cloud. Planners utilize numerous remote correspondence frameworks like (BLE 4.0), ZigBee, ESP43 Wi-Fi Modules,

433MHz RF Modules, Lora, nRF and so forth, and the determination of medium relies upon the kind of use it is being utilized in.

Among every one of the, one well known remote mechanism for nearby organize correspondence is the nRF24L01. These modules work on 2.4GHz (ISM band) with baud rate from 250Kbps to 2Mbps which is legitimate in numerous nations and can be utilized in modern and medicinal applications. It is additionally guaranteed that with appropriate radio wires these modules can transmit and get up to a separation of 100 meters between them. Fascinating right!!? Along these lines, in this instructional exercise we will get familiar with these nRF24l01 modules and how to interface it with a microcontroller stage like Arduino. We will likewise share a few answers for the ordinarily confronted issues while utilizing this module.

Getting to know the nRF24L01 RF Module

The nRF24L01 modules are handset modules, which means every module can send as well as get information since they are half-duplex they can either send or get information at once. The module has the non-exclusive nRF24L01 IC from Nordic semi-conductors which is in charge of transmission and gathering of information. The IC conveys utilizing the SPI convention and subsequently can be effectively interfaced with any microcontrollers. It gets much simpler with Arduino since the libraries are promptly accessible.

The pinouts of a standard nRF24L01 module is demonstrated as follows

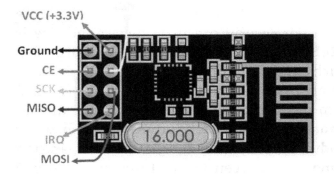

The module has on working voltage from 1.9V to 3.6V (commonly 3.3V) and devours less present of just 12mA during typical activity which makes it battery proficient and henceforth can even keep running on coin cells. In case the working voltage is 3.3V the majority of the pins are 5V tolerant and thus can be legitimately interfaced with 5V microcontrollers like Arduino. Another bit of leeway of utilizing these modules is, every module contains 6 Pipelines. Which means, every module can speak with 6 different modules to transmit or else get information. This makes the module appropriate for making star or work organizes in IoT applications. Additionally, they have a wide address scope of 125 interesting ID's, subsequently in a shut territory we can utilize 125 of these modules without meddling with one another.

Interfacing nRF24L01 with Arduino

In this project we will learn how to interface the nRF24L01 with Arduino by controlling the servo engine associated with one Arduino by shifting the potentiometer on the other Arduino. For effortlessness we have utilized one nRF24L01 module as transmitter and the other is recipient, however every module can be modified to send and get information exclusively.

The circuit graph to interface the nRF24L01 module with Arduino is demonstrated as follows. For Varity, I utilized the UNO for the recipient side and Nano for the transmitter side. Be that as it may, the rationale for association continues as before for other Arduino sheets like smaller than expected, mega too.

Receiver side: Arduino Uno nRF24L01 module connections

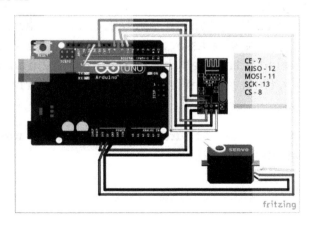

As said before the nRF24L01 speaks with the assistance of SPI convention. On Arduino Nano and UNO, the pins 11, 12 and 13 are utilized for SPI correspondence. Subsequently we interface the MOSI, MISO as well as SCK pins from nRF to the pins 11, 12 as well as 13 individually. The pins CE and CS are client configurable, I have utilized stick 7 and 8 here, yet you can utilize any stick by modifying the program. The nRF module is controlled by the 3.3V stick on Arduino, which by and large will work. If not, a different power supply can be attempted. Aside from interfacing the nRF I have likewise associated a servo engine to stick 7 and fueled it through the 5V stick on Arduino. Additionally, the transmitter circuit is demonstrated as follows.

Transmitter side: Arduino Nano nRF24L01 module Connections

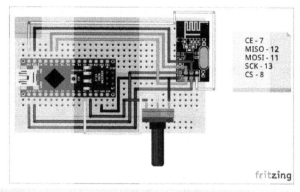

CE - 7
MISO - 12
MOSI - 11
SCK - 13
CS - 8

fritzing

The associations for the transmitter is likewise the equivalent, moreover I have utilized a potentiometer associated over the 5V promotion Ground stick of Arduino. The yield simple voltage which will change from 0-5V is associated with the A7 stick of the Nano. Both the sheets are controlled through the USB port.

Working with nRF24L01+ Wireless Transceiver Module

Anyway so as to make our nRF24L01 to work free from clamor we should think about the accompanying things. I have been taking a shot at this nRF24L01+ for quite a while and took in the accompanying focuses which can help you from getting hit on a divider. You can attempt these when the modules did not work the ordinary way.

1. The vast majority of the nRF24L01+ modules in the market are phony. The shabby ones that we can discover on Ebay and Amazon are the most exceedingly awful (Don't stress, with few changes we can make them work)

2. The primary issue is the power supply, not your code. The greater part of the codes online will work appropriately, I myself have a working code which I for one tried, let me know whether you need them.

3. Focus in light of the fact that the modules which are printed as NRF24L01+ are really Si24Ri (Yes a Chinese item).

4. The clone and phony modules will expend more power, consequently don't build up your capacity circuit dependent on nRF24L01+ datasheet, in light of the fact that Si24Ri will have high current utiliza-

tion about 250mA.

5. Be careful with Voltage swells and current floods, these modules are extremely delicate and may effectively catch fire. (;- (singed up 2 modules up until this point)

6. Including a few capacitors (10uF and 0.1uF) crosswise over Vcc and Gnd of the module helps in making your stockpile unadulterated and this works for a large portion of the modules.

Still in the event that you have issues report on remark segment or read through this, or pose your inquiries on our discussion.
Additionally, check our pervious venture on making a Chat room utilizing nRF24L01.

Programming nRF24L01 for Arduino

It has been exceptionally simple to utilize these modules with Arduino, because of the promptly accessible library made by maniac bug on GitHub. Snap on the connection to download the library as ZIP envelope and add it to your Arduino IDE by utilizing the Sketch - > Include Library - > Add .ZIP library alternative. Subsequent to including the library we can start programming for task. We need to compose two projects; one is for the transmitter side as well as the other for collector side. Anyway as I told before every module can work both as a transmitter and beneficiary. Both the projects are given toward the part of the arrangement, in the transmitter code the recipient alternative will be remarked out and in the beneficiary program the transmitter code will be remarked out. You can utilize it in case you are attempting a venture where the module needs to fill in as both. The working of the program is clarified beneath.

Like all projects we start by including the header documents. Since the nRF utilizes SPI convention we have incorporated the SPI header and furthermore the library that we just downloaded. The servo library is utilized to control the servo engine.

```
#include <SPI.h>

#include "RF24.h"

#include <Servo.h>
```

The following line is the significant line where we train the library about the CE and CS pins. In our circuit outline we have associated CE to stick 7 and CS to stick 8 so we set the line as

```
RF24 myRadio (7, 8);
```

Every one of the factors that are related with the

RF library ought to be proclaimed as a composite variable structure. In this program the variable msg is utilized to send and get information from the RF module.

```
struct package

{

  int msg;

};

typedef struct package Package;

Package data;
```

Every RF module has a one of a kind location utilizing which it can send information to the particular gadget. Since we are having just one sets here, we set the location to focus in both transmitter and collector yet on the off chance that you have various module you can set the ID to any exceptional 6 digit string.

```
byte addresses[][6] = {"0"};
```

Next inside the void arrangement work we introduce

the RF module and set to work with 115 band which
is free from clamor and furthermore set the module
to work in least control utilization mode with least
speed of 250Kbps.

```
void setup()

{

    Serial.begin(9600);

    myRadio.begin();

    myRadio.setChannel(115);    //115 band above
    WIFI signals

    myRadio.setPALevel(RF24_PA_MIN);    //MIN
    power low rage

    myRadio.setDataRate( RF24_250KBPS );  //Min-
    imum speed

    myservo.attach(6);

    Serial.print("Setup Initialized");

    delay(500);

}
```

void WriteData() work composes the information go to it. As told before the nRF has 6 distinct channels to which we can peruse or compose information, here we have utilized 0xF0F0F0F066 as location to compose information. On the collector side we need to utilize a similar location on ReadData() capacity to get the information that was composed.

```
void WriteData()

{

    myRadio.stopListening(); //Stop Receiving and
start transminitng

    myRadio.openWritingPipe(0xF0F0F0F066);//
Sends data on this 40-bit address

    myRadio.write(&data, sizeof(data));

    delay(300);

}
```

void WriteData() work peruses the information and places it in a variable. Again out of 6 distinct funnels utilizing which we can peruse or compose information here we have utilized 0xF0F0F0F0AA as location to peruse information. This implies the transmitter of the other module has composed something on this location and henceforth we are understanding it from the equivalent.

```
void ReadData()

{

myRadio.openReadingPipe(1, 0xF0F0F0F0AA); //
Which pipe to read, 40 bit Address

    myRadio.startListening(); //Stop Transminting
and start Reveicing

    if ( myRadio.available())

    {

        while (myRadio.available())

        {

            myRadio.read( &data, sizeof(data) );

        }

        Serial.println(data.text);

    }
```

}

Aside from these lines different lines in the program are utilized for perusing the POT and changing over it to 0 to 180 utilizing guide work and send it to the Receiver module where we control the servo as needs be. I have not clarified them line by line since we have as of now discovered that in our Servo Interfacing instructional exercise.

Controlling Servo Motor using nRF24L01 wirelessly

When you are prepared with the program transfer the transmitter and collector code (given beneath) on particular Arduino barricades and power them with USB port. You can likewise dispatch the sequential screen of both the sheets to check what worth is being transmitted and what is being gotten. In the event that everything is filling in true to form when you turn the POT handle on transmitter side the servo on the opposite side ought to likewise turn as needs be.

It is very typical for not getting these modules to take a shot from the start attempt, If you have confronted any issue check the code and wiring again and attempt the above given issue shooting rules. On the off chance that nothing works post your concern on the discussions or in the remark segment and I will attempt to determine them.

Code

Code for Transmitter Part:

```
/*Transmit POT value through NRF24L01 using Arduino
*
* Pin Conections
* CE - 7
  MISO - 12
  MOSI - 11
  SCK - 13
  CS - 8
  POT-A7
*/
#include <SPI.h>
#include "RF24.h"
RF24 myRadio (7, 8);
struct package
{
 int msg = 0;
};
byte addresses[][6] = {"0"};
```

```
typedef struct package Package;
Package data;
void setup()
{
 Serial.begin(9600);
 myRadio.begin();
  myRadio.setChannel(115);  //115 band above WIFI
signals
   myRadio.setPALevel(RF24_PA_MIN); //MIN power
low rage
   myRadio.setDataRate( RF24_250KBPS ) ;  //Min-
imum speed
 delay(500);
 Serial.print("Setup Initialized");
}
void loop()
{
 int Read_ADC = analogRead(A7);
 char servo_value = map (Read_ADC, 0, 1024, 0,180);
  if(servo_value>1)
  data.msg = servo_value;
  WriteData();
  delay(50);
// ReadData();
//delay(200);
}
void WriteData()
{
 myRadio.stopListening(); //Stop Receiving and start
transminitng
```

```
    myRadio.openWritingPipe( 0xF0F0F0F0AA); //
Sends data on this 40-bit address
 myRadio.write(&data, sizeof(data));
Serial.print("\nSent:");
 Serial.println(data.msg);
 delay(300);
}
void ReadData()
{
myRadio.openReadingPipe(1,   0xF0F0F0F066);  //
Which pipe to read, 40 bit Address
 myRadio.startListening(); //Stop Transminting and
start Reveicing
 if( myRadio.available())
 {
  while (myRadio.available())
  {
   myRadio.read( &data, sizeof(data) );
  }
  Serial.print("\nReceived:");
  Serial.println(data.msg);
 }
}
```

Code for Receiver Part:

```
/*CE - 7
MISO - 12
MOSI - 11
SCK - 13
CS - 8
Recently tested with nano
```

```
*/
#include <SPI.h>
#include "RF24.h"
#include <Servo.h>
Servo myservo;
RF24 myRadio (7, 8);
struct package
{
 int msg;
};
typedef struct package Package;
Package data;
byte addresses[][6] = {"0"};
void setup()
{
 Serial.begin(9600);
 myRadio.begin();
  myRadio.setChannel(115);  //115 band above WIFI
signals
  myRadio.setPALevel(RF24_PA_MIN); //MIN power
low rage
  myRadio.setDataRate( RF24_250KBPS ) ;  //Min-
imum speed
 myservo.attach(6);

  Serial.print("Setup Initialized");
 delay(500);
}
int Servo_value;
```

```
int Pev_servo_value;
void loop()
{
ReadData();
delay(50);


 Pev_servo_value = Servo_value;
 Servo_value = data.msg;
  while (Pev_servo_value< Servo_value)
 {
 myservo.write(Pev_servo_value);
 Pev_servo_value++;
 delay(2);
 }
 while (Pev_servo_value> Servo_value)
 {
 myservo.write(Pev_servo_value);
 Pev_servo_value--;
 delay(2);
 }
  //data.msg = "nothing to send";
 //WriteData();
 // delay(50);
}
void ReadData()
{
  myRadio.openReadingPipe(1, 0xF0F0F0F0AA); //
Which pipe to read, 40 bit Address
  myRadio.startListening(); //Stop Transminting and
```

```
start Reveicing
  if( myRadio.available())
 {
  while (myRadio.available())
  {
   myRadio.read( &data, sizeof(data) );
  }
  Serial.print("\nReceived:");
  Serial.println(data.msg);
 }
}
void WriteData()
{
 myRadio.stopListening(); //Stop Receiving and start
transminitng
 myRadio.openWritingPipe(0xF0F0F0F066);//Sends
data on this 40-bit address
 myRadio.write(&data, sizeof(data));
 Serial.print("\nSent:");
 Serial.println(data.msg);
 delay(300);
}
```

4.ARDUINO BASED GUITAR TUNER

Greetings folks, during the most recent couple of weeks, I've been taking a shot at reconnecting with my affection for the guitar. Playing the crate guitar was the means by which I loosen up couple of years back before the saxophone dominated. Back to the guitar, following 3 years of once in a while strumming a harmony, I found in addition to other things that I never again knew how every one of the string should sound, to place it in my companion's words, "My hearing was never again tuned" and accordingly, I was not ready to tune the guitar without the guide of a console or a versatile application which I later downloaded. The weeks passed by till couple of days prior when the producer in me ended up persuaded and I chose to fabricate an Arduino based Guitar Tuner. In the present instructional exercise, I will share how to manufacture your own DIY Arduino Guitar Tuner.

How Guitar Tuner Works

Before we move to the hardware, its essential to comprehend the standard behind the construct. There are 7 noteworthy melodic notes signified by the letters in order; A, B, C, D, E, F, G and more often than not end with another A which is consistently at an octet higher than the initial A. In music a few forms of these notes exists like the initial An and the last A. These notes are recognized every one from their variety and from each other by one of the qualities of sound known as pitch. Pitch is characterized as the din or lowness of sound and its shown by the recurrence of that sound. Since the recurrence of these notes are known, for us to decide whether the guitar is tuned or not, we just need to look at the recurrence of the note of specific string to the genuine recurrence of the note that the string speaks to.

The frequencies of the 7 melodic notes are:

A = 27.50Hz

B = 30.87Hz

C = 16.35Hz

D = 18.35Hz

E = 20.60Hz

F = 21.83Hz

G = 24.50 Hz

Every variety of these notes is consistently at a pitch equivalent to FxM where F is the recurrence and M is a non-zero whole number. Along these lines for the last A which as depicted before, is at an octet higher than the initial A, the recurrence is;

27.50 x 2 = 55Hz.

The guitar (Lead/box guitar) normally has 6 strings indicated by the notes E, A, D, G, B, E on open string. Of course, last E will be at an octet higher than the main E. We will plan our guitar tuner to help tune the guitar utilizing the frequencies of these notes.

As indicated by the standard guitar tuning, the note and relating recurrence of each string is appeared in the table beneath.

Strings	Frequency	Notation

1 (E)	329.63 Hz	E4
2 (B)	246.94 Hz	B3
3 (G)	196.00 Hz	G3
4 (D)	146.83 Hz	D3
5 (A)	110.00 Hz	A2
6 (E)	82.41 Hz	E2

The venture stream is very basic; we convert the sound sign created by the guitar to a recurrence at that point contrast and the precise recurrence estimation of the string being tuned. The guitarist is told utilizing a LED when the worth relates.

The recurrence location/change includes 3 fundamental stages;

- Intensifying

- Counterbalancing

- Simple to Digital conversion(sampling)

The sound sign being delivered will be unreasonably feeble for the Arduino's ADC to perceive so we have to enhance the sign. After enhancement, to keep the sign inside the range conspicuous by the Arduino's ADC to counteract cutting of the sign, we counterbalance the voltage of the sign. In the wake of balancing, the sign is then passed to the Arduino ADC where it is examined and the recurrence of that sound is gotten.

Required components

The accompanying parts are required to manufacture this undertaking;

1. Condenser Mic x1

2. LM386 x1

3. Arduino Uno x1

4. Mouthpiece/Audio jack x1

5. O.1uf capacitor x2

6. 5mm green LED x1

7. 10k potentiometer x1

8. 10ohms resistor x1

9. 100ohms resistor x4

10. 5mm yellow LED x2

11. 10uf capacitor x3

12. Regularly Open Push Buttons x6

13. Breadboard

14. Jumper wires

Schematics

Interface the parts as appeared in the Guitar Tuner Circuit Diagram underneath.

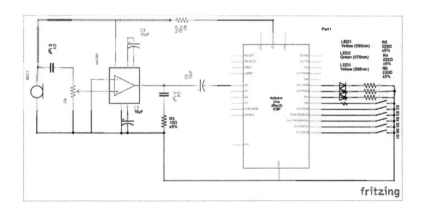

The push catches are associated without draw up/down resistors on the grounds that the Arduino's in manufactured pullup resistors will be utilized. This is to guarantee the circuit is as straightforward as could reasonably be expected.

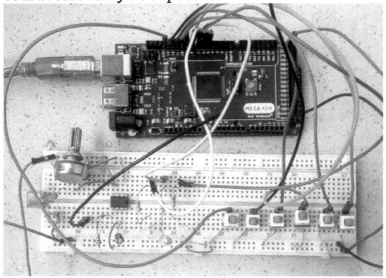

Arduino Code for Guitar Tuner

The calculation behind the code for this Guitar Tuner Project is basic. To tune a specific string, the guitarist chooses the string by squeezing the comparing pushbutton and strums the plays an open string. The sound is gathered by the intensification organize and passed on to the Arduino ADC. The recurrence is decoded and thought about. At the point when the information recurrence from the string is not actually the predefined recurrence, for that string one of the yellow LEDs please demonstrating that the string should be fixed. At the point when the deliberate recurrence is more noteworthy than the stipulated recurrence for that string, another LED goes ahead. At the point when the recurrence is inside the stipulated range for that string the green LED makes advances on guide the guitarist.

Complete Arduino code is given toward the end, here we have quickly clarified the significant pieces of code.

We start by making an exhibit to hold the switches.

```
int buttonarray[] = {13, 12, 11, 10, 9, 8}; // [E2, A2,
D3, G3, B3, E4]
```

Next, we make a cluster to hold the comparing recurrence for every one of the strings.

```
float freqarray[] = {82.41, 110.00, 146.83, 196.00,
246.94, 329.63};//all in Hz
```

With this done, we at that point pronounce the pins to which the LEDs are associated and different factors that will be utilized for getting the recurrence from the ADC.

```
int lowerLed = 7;

int higherLed = 6;

int justRight = 5;

#define LENGTH 512

byte rawData[LENGTH];

int count;
```

Next is the void arrangement() work.

Here we start by empowering the inner draw up on the Arduino for every one of the pins to which the switches is associated. After which we set the pins to which the LEDs are associated as yields and dispatch the sequential screen to show the information.

```
void setup()

{

  for (int i=0; i<=5; i++)

  {
```

```
   pinMode(buttonarray[i], INPUT_PULLUP);

}

pinMode(lowerLed, OUTPUT);

pinMode(higherLed, OUTPUT);

pinMode(justRight, OUTPUT);

Serial.begin(115200);

}
```

Next, is the void circle work, we actualize the recurrence recognition and examination.

```
void loop(){

if (count < LENGTH)

{

  count++;

  rawData[count] = analogRead(A0)>>2;

}
```

```
else {

  sum = 0;

  pd_state = 0;

  int period = 0;

  for(i=0; i < len; i++)

  {

    // Autocorrelation

    sum_old = sum;

    sum = 0;

    for(k=0;  k  <  len-i;  k++)  sum  +=
(rawData[k]-128)*(rawData[k+i]-128)/256;

    // Serial.println(sum);

    // Peak Detect State Machine

    if (pd_state == 2 && (sum-sum_old) <=0)

    {

      period = i;
```

```
    pd_state = 3;

}

    if (pd_state == 1 && (sum > thresh) && (sum-
sum_old) > 0) pd_state = 2;

    if (!i) {

      thresh = sum * 0.5;

      pd_state = 1;

    }

}

    // Frequency identified in Hz

    if (thresh > 100) {

      freq_per = sample_freq/period;

      Serial.println(freq_per);

      for (int s=0; s<=5; s++)

      {

        if (digitalRead(buttonarray[i])== HIGH)
```

```
{

    if (freq_per - freqarray[i] < 0)

    {

    digitalWrite(lowerLed, HIGH);

    }

    else if(freq_per - freqarray[i] > 10)

    {

    digitalWrite(higherLed, HIGH);

    }

    else

    {

    digitalWrite(justRight, HIGH);

    }

    }

}
```

```
    }

    count = 0;

  }

}
```

The total code is given beneath. Transfer the code to your Arduino board as well as strum away.

Code

```
int buttonarray[] = {13, 12, 11, 10, 9, 8}; // [E2, A2, D3, G3, B3, E4]
// each pin represents a guitar string
// next we create and array with frequencies matching each of the strings above
// such that when 13 is selected the freq matching the note e is selected).
float freqarray[] = {82.41, 110.00, 146.83, 196.00, 246.94, 329.63};//sll in Hz
int lowerLed = 7;
int higherLed = 6;
int justRight = 5;
#define LENGTH 512
byte rawData[LENGTH];
int count = 0;
// Sample Frequency in kHz
const float sample_freq = 8919;
```

```
int len = sizeof(rawData);
int i,k;
long sum, sum_old;
int thresh = 0;
float freq_per = 0;
byte pd_state = 0;
void setup(){
 for (int i=0; i<=5; i++)
 {
  pinMode(buttonarray[i], INPUT_PULLUP);
 }
 pinMode(lowerLed, OUTPUT);
 pinMode(higherLed, OUTPUT);
 pinMode(justRight, OUTPUT);
 Serial.begin(115200);
}
void loop(){

 if(count < LENGTH)
 {
 count++;
 rawData[count] = analogRead(A0)>>2;
 }
 else {
  sum = 0;
  pd_state = 0;
  int period = 0;
  for(i=0; i < len; i++)
  {
   // Autocorrelation
```

```
sum_old = sum;
sum = 0;
        for(k=0;  k  <  len-i;  k++)  sum  +=
(rawData[k]-128)*(rawData[k+i]-128)/256;
// Serial.println(sum);


  // Peak Detect State Machine
if(pd_state == 2 && (sum-sum_old) <=0)
{
 period = i;
 pd_state = 3;
}
   if (pd_state == 1 && (sum > thresh) && (sum-
sum_old) > 0) pd_state = 2;
 if(!i) {
 thresh = sum * 0.5;
  pd_state = 1;
 }
}
// Frequency identified in Hz
if(thresh > 100) {
 freq_per = sample_freq/period;
 Serial.println(freq_per);
 for (int s=0; s<=5; s++)
 {
  if(digitalRead(buttonarray[i])== HIGH)
  {
   if(freq_per - freqarray[i] < 0)
   {
    digitalWrite(lowerLed, HIGH);
```

```
    }
    else if(freq_per - freqarray[i] > 10)
    {
     digitalWrite(higherLed, HIGH);
    }
    else
    {
     digitalWrite(justRight, HIGH);
    }


      }
   }
  }
  count = 0;
 }
}
```

5.ANALOG SPEEDOMETER USING ARDUINO AND IR SENSOR

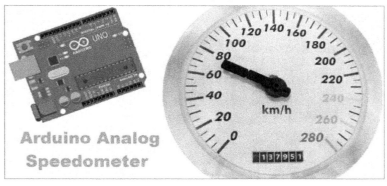

Estimating the speed/rpm of a Vehicle or an engine has consistently been an interesting venture to attempt. In this task, we are gonna to construct an Analog Speedometer utilizing the Arduino. We will utilize IR Sensor module to gauge the speed. There are different ways/sensors for this, similar to lobby sensor to quantify speed, however utilizing an IR sensor is simple since IR sensor module is basic gadget and we can get it effectively from the market and furthermore it may be utilized on an engine/Vehicle.

In this task, we are gonna to show speed in both simple and advanced structure. By doing this venture, we will likewise improve our aptitudes in learning Arduino and Stepper engine since this undertaking includes utilization of Interrupts and Timers. At, the part of the bargain you will most likely compute the speed and separations secured by any pivoting item and show them on a 16x2 LCD screen in computerized group and furthermore on simple meter. So how about we start with this Speedometer as well as Odometer Circuit with Arduino

Materials Required

1. A bipolar stepper engine (4 wire)

2. Arduino

3. IR sensor module

4. Stepper engine driver (L298n Module)

5. 2.2k resistor

6. 16*2 LCD show

7. Breadboard.

8. Associating wires

9. Speedometer picture printout

10. Power supply

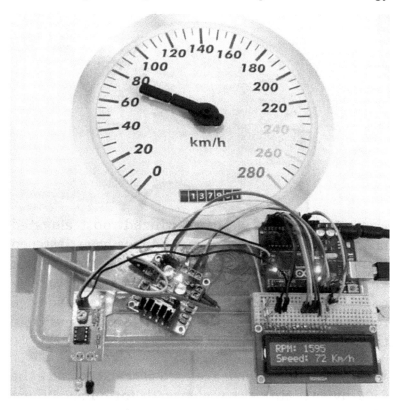

Calculating Speed and Showing it on Analog Speedometer

An IR Sensor is a gadget which can distinguish the nearness of an article before it. We have utilized two sharp edge rotor (fan) and set the IR sensor close to it so that each time the cutting edges pivot the IR sensor identifies it. We at that point utilize the assistance of clocks and Interrupts in Arduino to compute the time taken for one complete pivot of the engine.

Here in this task, we have utilized most elevated need hinder to recognize rpm and we have designed it in rising mode. So that at whatever point sensor yield goes LOW to High, work RPMCount() will be executed. What's more, as we have utilized two edge rotor, It implies the capacity will be called multiple times in a single transformation.

When the time taken is realized we can compute the RPM by utilizing the underneath formulae, Where 1000/time taken will give us the RPS (unrest every second) and further duplicating it with 60 will give you the RPM (insurgency every moment)

```
rpm = (60/2)*(1000/(millis() - time))*REV/bla-
desInFan;
```

In the wake of getting RPM, speed can be determined by given recipe:

Speed = rpm * (2 * Pi * radius) / 1000

We realize that Pi = 3.14 and sweep is 4.7 inch

Be that as it may, first we have to change over sweep into meters from inches:

radius = ((radius * 2.54)/100.0) meters

Speed= rpm * 60.0 * (2.0 * 3.14 * radius)/ 1000.0) in kilometers per hour

Here we have duplicated rpm by 60 to change over rpm to rph (upset every hour) and partitioned by 1000 to change over meters/hour to Kilometers/hour.

In the wake of having speed in kmh we can demonstrate these qualities legitimately over the LCD in computerized structure yet to show speed in the simple structure we have to do one more computation to discover no. of steps, stepper engine should move to show speed on simple meter.

Here we have utilized a 4 wire bipolar stepper engine for simple meter, which is having 1.8 degree implies 200 stages for every insurgency.

Presently we need to demonstrate 280 Kmh on speed-ometer. So to indicate 280 Kmh stepper engine needs to move 280 degree

So we have maxSpeed = 280

Also, maxSteps will be

maxSteps = 280/1.8 = 155 steps

Presently we have a capacity in our Arduino code in particular guide work which is utilized here to guide speed into steps.

> **Steps = map(speed,0,maxSpeed,0,maxSteps);**

So now we have

> **steps=map(speed,0,280,0,155);**

Subsequent to ascertaining steps we can straightforwardly apply these means in stepper engine capacity to move stepper engine. We additionally need to deal with current advances or point of the stepper engine by utilizing given figurings

> **currSteps=Steps**
>
> **steps= currSteps-preSteps**
>
> **preSteps=currSteps**

here currSteps is current advances that is originating from last count and preSteps is last performed advances.

Circuit Diagram and Connections

Circuit outline for this Analog Speedometer is basic, here we have utilized 16x2 LCD to show speed in computerized structure and stepper engine to pivot the simple speedometer needle.

16x2 LCD is associated at following simple pins of Arduino.

RS - A5

RW - GND

EN - A4

D4 - A3

D5 - A2

D6 - A1

D7 - A0

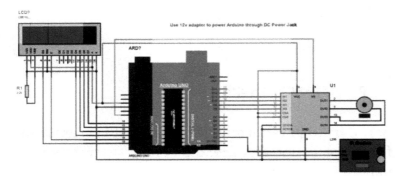

A 2.2k resistor is utilized to set the splendor of LCD. An IR sensor module, which is utilized to recognize fan's edge to compute the rpm, is associated with intrude on 0 methods D2 stick of Arduino.

Here we have utilized a stepper engine driver in particular L293N module. IN1, IN2, IN3 and IN4 stick of stepper engine driver is straightforwardly associated with D8, D9, D10, and D11 of Arduino. Rest of associations are given in Circuit Diagram.

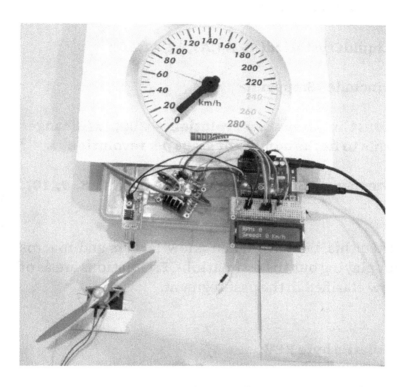

Programming Explanation

Complete code for Arduino Speedometer is given toward the end, here we are clarifying couple of significant piece of it.

In programming part, we have incorporated all the

required libraries like stepper engine library, Liquid-Crystal LCD library and pronounced pins for them.

```
#include<LiquidCrystal.h>

LiquidCrystal lcd(A5,A4,A3,A2,A1,A0);

#include <Stepper.h>

const int stepsPerRevolution = 200;  // change
this to fit the number of steps per revolution

Stepper myStepper(stepsPerRevolution, 8, 9, 10,
11);
```

After this, we have taken a few factors and macros for playing out the estimations. Estimations are as of now clarified in the past segment.

```
volatile byte REV;

unsigned long int rpm,RPM;

unsigned long st=0;

unsigned long time;

int ledPin = 13;
```

```
int led = 0,RPMlen , prevRPM;

int flag = 0;

int flag1=1;

#define bladesInFan 2

float radius=4.7;  // inch

int preSteps=0;

float   stepAngle=   360.0/(float)stepsPerRevolu-
tion;

float minSpeed=0;

float maxSpeed=280.0;

float minSteps=0;

float maxSteps=maxSpeed/stepAngle;
```

After this, we instate the LCD, Serial, hinder and Stepper engine in the arrangement work

```
void setup()

{
```

```
myStepper.setSpeed(60);

Serial.begin(9600);

pinMode(ledPin, OUTPUT);

lcd.begin(16,2);

lcd.print("Speedometer");

delay(2000);

attachInterrupt(0, RPMCount, RISING);

}
```

After this, we read rpm in circle work and play out a computation to get speed and convert that into steps to run stepper engine to show speed in simple structure.

```
void loop()

{

   readRPM();

   radius=((radius * 2.54)/100.0);  // convering in
meter
```

```
int Speed= ((float)RPM * 60.0 * (2.0 * 3.14 * ra-
dius)/1000.0);

// RPM in 60 minute, diameter of tyre (2pi r) r is
radius, 1000 to convert in km

int      Steps=map(Speed,      minSpeed,max-
Speed,minSteps,maxSteps);

if(flag1)

{

Serial.print(Speed);

Serial.println("Kmh");

lcd.setCursor(0,0);

lcd.print("RPM: ");

lcd.print(RPM);

lcd.print("     ");

lcd.setCursor(0,1);

lcd.print("Speed: ");

lcd.print(Speed);
```

```
   lcd.print(" Km/h    ");

   flag1=0;

 }

   int currSteps=Steps;

   int steps= currSteps-preSteps;

   preSteps=currSteps;

   myStepper.step(steps);

}
```

Here we have reapRPM() capacity to compute RPM.

```
int readRPM()

{

   if(REV >= 10 or millis()>=st+1000)        // IT
WILL UPDATE AFETR EVERY 10 READINGS or 1
second in idle

   {

     if(flag==0)
```

```
flag=1;

rpm = (60/2)*(1000/(millis() - time))*REV/bladesInFan;

time = millis();

REV = 0;

int x= rpm;

while(x!=0)

{

x = x/10;

RPMlen++;

}

Serial.println(rpm,DEC);

RPM=rpm;

delay(500);

st=millis();

flag1=1;
```

```
    }

}
```

At long last, we have interfere with routine which is dependable to quantify upset of article

```
void RPMCount()

{

  REV++;

  if (led == LOW)

  {

    led = HIGH;

  }

  else

  {

    led = LOW;

  }
```

```
    digitalWrite(ledPin, led);

}
```

This is the way you can basically construct an Analog Speedometer utilizing Arduino. This can be additionally fabricated utilizing Hall sensor and speed can be shown on advanced mobile phone, pursue this Arduino Speedometer instructional exercise for the equivalent.

Code
```
#include<LiquidCrystal.h>
LiquidCrystal lcd(A5,A4,A3,A2,A1,A0);
#include <Stepper.h>
const int stepsPerRevolution = 200; // change this to
fit the number of steps per revolution
Stepper myStepper(stepsPerRevolution, 8, 9, 10, 11);
volatile byte REV;
unsigned long int rpm,RPM;
unsigned long st=0;
unsigned long time;
int ledPin = 13;
int led = 0,RPMlen , prevRPM;
int flag = 0;
int flag1 = 1;
#define bladesInFan 2
float radius=4.7; //inch
int preSteps=0;
float stepAngle= 360.0/(float)stepsPerRevolution;
```

```
float minSpeed=0;
float maxSpeed=280.0;
float minSteps=0;
float maxSteps=maxSpeed/stepAngle;
void setup()
{
  myStepper.setSpeed(60);
  Serial.begin(9600);
  pinMode(ledPin, OUTPUT);
  lcd.begin(16,2);
  lcd.print("Speedometer");
  delay(2000);
  attachInterrupt(0, RPMCount, RISING);
}
void loop()
{
  readRPM();
  radius=((radius*2.54)/100.0); // converingin meter
    int Speed= ((float)RPM * 60.0 * (2.0 * 3.14 * ra-
dius)/1000.0);
    // RPM in 60 minute, diameter of tyre (2pi r) r is ra-
dius, 1000 to convert in km
    int Steps=map(Speed, minSpeed,maxSpeed,min-
Steps,maxSteps);

  if(flag1)
  {
  Serial.print(Speed);
  Serial.println("Kmh");
  lcd.setCursor(0,0);
```

```
lcd.print("RPM: ");
lcd.print(RPM);
lcd.print("      ");
lcd.setCursor(0,1);
lcd.print("Speed: ");
lcd.print(Speed);
lcd.print(" Km/h    ");
flag1=0;
}
int currSteps=Steps;
int steps= currSteps-preSteps;
preSteps=currSteps;
myStepper.step(steps);
}
int readRPM()
{
if(REV >= 10 or millis()>=st+1000)        // IT WILL
UPDATE AFETR EVERY 10 READINGS or 1 second in
idle
{
  if(flag==0)
   flag=1;
  rpm = (60/2)*(1000/(millis() - time))*REV/bladesIn-
Fan;
  time = millis();
  REV = 0;
  int x= rpm;
  while(x!=0)
  {
   x = x/10;
   RPMlen++;
```

```
   }
   Serial.println(rpm,DEC);
   RPM=rpm;
   delay(500);
   st=millis();
   flag1=1;
  }
}
void RPMCount()
{
 REV++;
 if(led == LOW)
 {
  led = HIGH;
 }
 else
 {
  led = LOW;
 }
 digitalWrite(ledPin, led);
}
```

6.LC METER USING ARDUINO: MEASURING INDUCTANCE AND FREQUENCY

Every single installed sweetheart know about multimeter which an incredible device to gauge voltage, current, opposition and so forth. A multimeter can quantify them effectively. Be that as it may, in some cases we have to gauge inductance and capacitance which is unimaginable with an ordinary multimeter. There are some exceptional multimeters that can quantify inductance and capacitance yet they are expensive. We effectively constructed Frequency Meter, Capacitance Meter and Resistance meter utilizing Arduino. Here we are gonna to make an Inductance LC Meter utilizing Arduino. In this venture, we will demonstrate the inductance and capacitance esteems alongside the recurrence over 16x2 LCD show. A push catch is given in the circuit, to switch among capacitance and inductance show.

Components Required

1. Arduino Uno
2. 3v battery
3. 741 opamp IC
4. Capacitors
5. 100-ohm resistor
6. 1n4007 diode
7. Inductors
8. 10k pot
9. 10k resistor
10. Push button
11. Power supply
12. Connecting wires
13. Breadboard or PCB

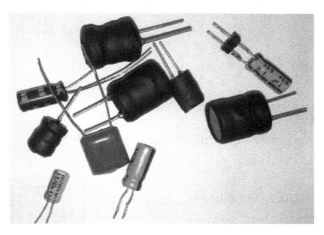

Calculating Frequency and Inductance

In this venture we are going to gauge inductance and capacitance by utilizing a LC circuit in parallel. This circuit is a like a ring or chime which start resounding at certain recurrence. At whatever point we apply a heartbeat, this LC circuit will begin resounding and this reverberation recurrence is in type of simple (sinusoidal wave) so we have to change over it in squire wave. To do this, we apply this simple reverberation recurrence to opamp (741 for our situation) that will change over it in squire wave (recurrence) at half of the obligation cycle. Presently we measure the recurrence by utilizing Arduino and by utilizing some scientific count we can discover the inductance or capacitance. We have utilized the given LC circuit recurrence reaction recipe.

f= 1 /(2*time)

where time is yield of pulseIn() work

presently we have LC circuit Frequency:

f= 1 /2*Pi* square root of (LC)

we can unravel it to get inductance:

f^2 = 1/ (4Pi^{2}LC)

L= 1/ (4Pi^{2}f^{2}C)

L = 1/(4* Pi * Pi * f * f * C)

As we previously referenced that our wave is sinus-oidal wave so it has a similar timeframe in both positive and negative plentifulness. Its methods the comparator will change over it into square wave having a half obligation cycle. With the goal that we can gauge it by utilizing pulseIn() capacity of Arduino. This capacity will give us a timespan which can be effectively changed over into a recurrence by rearranging the timeframe. As pulseIn capacity measure just one heartbeat, so now to get right recurrence we need to increase it by to 2. Presently we have a recurrence which can be changed over into inductance by utilizing the above recipe.

Note: while estimating inductance (L1), capacitor (C1) worth ought to be 0.1uF and keeping in mind that estimating capacitance (C1), inductor (L1) worth ought to be 10mH.

Circuit Diagram and Explanation

In this LC Meter circuit graph, we have utilized Arduino to control the task activity. In this, we have utilized a LC circuit. This LC circuit comprises of an Inductor and a capacitor. To change over sinusoidal reverberation recurrence to advanced or square wave we have utilized operational speaker to be specific 741. Here we have to apply negative stockpile to operation amp to get precise yield recurrence. So we have utilized a 3v battery associated backward extremity, implies 741 negative stick is associated with battery negative terminal and positive stick of the battery is associated with the ground of the rest of the circuit. For more explanation see the circuit outline underneath.

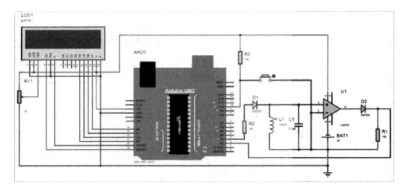

Here we have a push catch to change the method of activity whether we are estimating inductance or capacitance. A 16x2 LCD is utilized to demonstrate inductance or capacitance with the recurrence of LC circuit. A 10k pot is utilized for controlling the splendor of the LCD. Circuit is controlled with the support of Arduino 5v supply and we can control the Arduino by 5v utilizing USB or 12v connector.

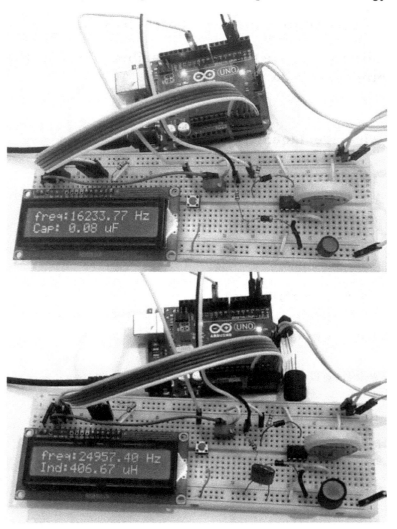

Programming Explanation

The programming some portion of this LC Meter undertaking is extremely simple. Complete Arduino code is given toward the part of the bargain.

Initially we have to incorporate library for LCD and pronounce a few pins and macros.

```
#include<LiquidCrystal.h>

LiquidCrystal lcd(A5, A4, A3, A2, A1, A0);

#define serial

#define charge 3

#define freqIn 2

#define mode 10

#define Delay 15

double frequency, capacitance, inductance;

typedef struct

{

  int flag: 1;

}Flag;
```

Flag Bit;

After it, in arrangement work we have introduced LCD and Serial correspondence to show estimated values over the LCD and sequential screen.

```
void setup()

{

#ifdef serial

  Serial.begin(9600);

#endif

  lcd.begin(16, 2);

  pinMode(freqIn, INPUT);

  pinMode(charge, OUTPUT);

  pinMode(mode, INPUT_PULLUP);

  lcd.print(" LC Meter Using ");

  lcd.setCursor(0, 1);

  lcd.print("   Arduino ");
```

```
delay(2000);

lcd.clear();

lcd.print("Hello_world");

delay(2000);

}
```

At that point in circle work, apply a beat of a fixed timeframe to LC circuit that will charge the LC circuit. In the wake of evacuating beat LC circuit starts resounding. At that point we read its square wave change, originating from operation amp, by utilizing pulseIn() capacity and convert that by duplicating by 2. Take few examples of this as well. That is the manner by which recurrence is determined:

```
void loop()

{

    for(int i=0;i<Delay;i++)

    {

        digitalWrite(charge, HIGH);
```

```
delayMicroseconds(100);

digitalWrite(charge, LOW);

delayMicroseconds(50);

double Pulse = pulseIn(freqIn, HIGH, 10000);

if (Pulse > 0.1)

  frequency+= 1.E6 / (2 * Pulse);

  delay(20);

}

frequency/=Delay;

#ifdef serial

Serial.print("frequency:");

Serial.print( frequency );

Serial.print(" Hz   ");

#endif

lcd.setCursor(0, 0);
```

```
lcd.print("freq:");

lcd.print( frequency );

lcd.print(" Hz   ");
```

In the wake of getting recurrence esteem, we have changed over them into inductance by utilizing given bit of code

```
capacitance = 0.1E-6;

inductance = (1. / (capacitance * frequency * fre-
quency * 4.*3.14159 * 3.14159)) * 1.E6;

#ifdef serial

Serial.print("Ind:");

if(inductance>=1000)

{

Serial.print( inductance/1000 );

Serial.println(" mH");

}
```

```
    else

  {

  Serial.print( inductance );

  Serial.println(" uH");

  }

#endif

  lcd.setCursor(0, 1);

  lcd.print("Ind:");

  if(inductance>=1000)

  {

  lcd.print( inductance/1000 );

  lcd.print(" mH      ");

  }

  else

  {
```

```
lcd.print( inductance );

lcd.print(" uH      ");

}

}
```

What's more, by utilizing given code we determined capacitance.

```
if (Bit.flag)

{

    inductance = 1.E-3;

    capacitance = ((1. / (inductance * frequency * fre-
quency * 4.*3.14159 * 3.14159)) * 1.E9);

    if((int)capacitance < 0)

    capacitance=0;

#ifdef serial

    Serial.print("Capacitance:");

    Serial.print( capacitance,6);
```

```
  Serial.println(" uF  ");

#endif

  lcd.setCursor(0, 1);

  lcd.print("Cap: ");

  if(capacitance > 47)

  {

   lcd.print( (capacitance/1000));

  lcd.print(" uF        ");

  }

  else

  {

   lcd.print(capacitance);

   lcd.print(" nF       ");

  }

}
```

So this is the means by which we determined recurrence, capacitance and Inductance utilizing Arduino and showed it on 16x2 LCD.

Code

```
#include<LiquidCrystal.h>
LiquidCrystal lcd(A5, A4, A3, A2, A1, A0);
#define serial
#define charge 3
#define freqIn 2
#define mode 10
#define Delay 15
double frequency, capacitance, inductance;
typedef struct
{
 int flag: 1;
}Flag;
Flag Bit;
void setup()
{
#ifdef serial
 Serial.begin(9600);
#endif
 lcd.begin(16, 2);
 pinMode(freqIn, INPUT);
 pinMode(charge, OUTPUT);
 pinMode(mode, INPUT_PULLUP);
 lcd.print(" LC Meter Using ");
 lcd.setCursor(0, 1);
```

```
lcd.print("  Arduino  ");
delay(2000);
lcd.clear();
lcd.print("Hello world");
delay(2000);
}
void loop()
{
 for(int i=0;i<Delay;i++)
 {
  digitalWrite(charge, HIGH);
  delayMicroseconds(100);
  digitalWrite(charge, LOW);
  delayMicroseconds(50);
 double Pulse = pulseIn(freqIn, HIGH, 10000);
 if(Pulse > 0.1)
  frequency+= 1.E6 / (2 * Pulse);
  delay(20);
 }
 frequency/=Delay;
#ifdef serial
 Serial.print("frequency:");
 Serial.print( frequency );
 Serial.print(" Hz  ");
#endif
  lcd.setCursor(0, 0);
 lcd.print("freq:");
 lcd.print( frequency );
 lcd.print(" Hz  ");
  if(Bit.flag)
```

```
{
  inductance = 1.E-3;
    capacitance = ((1. / (inductance * frequency * fre-
quency * 4.*3.14159 * 3.14159)) * 1.E9);
  if((int)capacitance < 0)
  capacitance=0;
#ifdef serial
  Serial.print("Capacitance:");
  Serial.print( capacitance,6);
  Serial.println(" uF ");
#endif
  lcd.setCursor(0, 1);
  lcd.print("Cap: ");
  if(capacitance > 47)
  {
   lcd.print( (capacitance/1000));
   lcd.print(" uF        ");
  }
  else
  {
   lcd.print(capacitance);
   lcd.print(" nF        ");
  }
}


  else
  {
  capacitance = 0.1E-6;
    inductance = (1. / (capacitance * frequency * fre-
quency * 4.*3.14159 * 3.14159)) * 1.E6;
```

```
#ifdef serial
  Serial.print("Ind:");
  if(inductance>=1000)
  {
  Serial.print( inductance/1000 );
  Serial.println(" mH");
  }
  else
  {
  Serial.print( inductance );
  Serial.println(" uH");
  }
#endif
    lcd.setCursor(0, 1);
  lcd.print("Ind:");
  if(inductance>=1000)
  {
  lcd.print( inductance/1000 );
  lcd.print(" mH        ");
  }
  else
  {
  lcd.print( inductance );
  lcd.print(" uH        ");
  }
  }
  if (digitalRead(mode) == LOW)
  {
  Bit.flag = !Bit.flag;
  delay(1000);
```

```
  while (digitalRead(mode) == LOW);
}
delay(50);
}
```

7.ARDUINO WATTMETER: MEASURE VOLTAGE, CURRENT AND POWER CONSUMPTION

As gadgets engineers, we generally rely on meters/instruments to gauge and break down the working of a circuit. Beginning with a basic multimeter to a mind boggling power quality analysers or DSOs everything has their very own exceptional applications. A vast portion of these meters are promptly accessible and can be obtained dependent on the parameters to be estimated and their precision. In any case, now and again we may finish in a circumstance where we have to fabricate our own meters. State for example you are chipping away at a sun powered PV venture and you might want to compute the power utilization of your heap, in such situations we can assemble our own Wattmeter utilizing a straightforward microcontroller stage like Arduino.

Building your very own meters cut down the expense of testing, yet in addition gives us space to facilitate the way toward testing. Like, a wattmeter assembled utilizing Arduino can without much of a stretch be changed to screen the outcomes on Serial screen and plot a chart on Serial plotter or add a SD card to naturally log the estimations of voltage, current and power at pre-characterized interims. Sounds intriguing right!? So we should begin...

Materials Required

1. LM358 Op-Amp

2. Arduino Nano

3. 7805 Voltage controller

4. 16*2 LCD show

5. 10k Trimmer pot

6. 0.22 ohm 2 Watt shunt resistor

7. 0.1uF Capacitors

8. 10k,20k,2.2k,1k Resistors

9. Test Load

10. Perf board or breadboard

11. Binding pack (discretionary)

Circuit Diagram

The total circuit graph of the arduino wattmeter venture is given underneath.

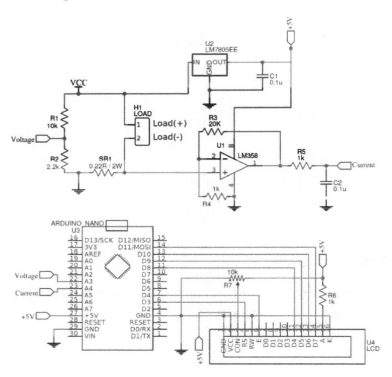

For simplicity of comprehension the arduino wattm-eter circuit is part into two units. The upper piece of the circuit is the estimating unit and the lower some portion of the circuit is the calculation and show unit. For individuals who are new to this sort of circuits pursued the marks. Model +5V is name which implies that every one of the pins to which mark is associated with ought to be considered as they are associated together. Marks are ordinarily used to make the circuit outline look slick.

The circuit is intended to fit into frameworks working between 0-24V with a present scope of 0-1A remembering the particular of a Solar PV. Without much of a stretch you can expand the range once you comprehend the working of the circuit. The hidden guideline behind the circuit is to gauge the voltage over the heap and current through it to figure the power devours by it. All the deliberate qualities will be shown in a 16*2 Alphanumeric LCD.

Further beneath we should part the circuit into little portions with the goal that we can get a reasonable picture of how the circuit is indented to function.

Measuring Unit

The estimating unit comprises of a potential divider to enable us to gauge the voltage and a shut resistor with a Non-Inverting Op-amp is utilized to enable us to quantify the current through the circuit. The potential divider part from the above circuit is demonstrated as follows

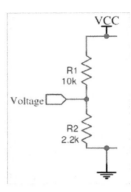

Here the Input voltage is speak to by Vcc, as told prior we are structuring the circuit for a voltage extend from 0V to 24V. In any case, a microcontroller like Arduino can't quantify such high estimations of voltage; it can just gauge voltage from 0-5V. So we need to outline the voltage scope of 0-24V to 0-5V. This can be effectively done by utilizing a potential divider circuit as demonstrated as follows. The resistor 10k and 2.2k together frames the potential divider circuit. The yield voltage of a potential divider can be determined utilizing the beneath formulae. The equivalent be utilized to choose the estimation of your resistors, you can utilize our online adding machine to figure estimation of resistor in the event that you are re-structuring the circuit.

Vout = (Vin × R2) / (R1 + R2)

The mapped 0-5V can be acquired from the center

part which is named as Voltage. This mapped voltage would then be able to be nourished to the Arduino Analog stick later.

Further we have to quantify the current through the LOAD. As we probably am aware microcontrollers can peruse just simple voltage, so we have to by one way or another proselyte the estimation of current to voltage. It very well may be finished by basically including a resistor (shunt resistor) in the way which as indicated by Ohm's law will drop an estimation of voltage crosswise over it that is corresponding to the present moving through it. The estimation of this voltage drop will be extremely less so we utilize an operation amp to enhance it. The circuit for the equivalent is demonstrated as follows

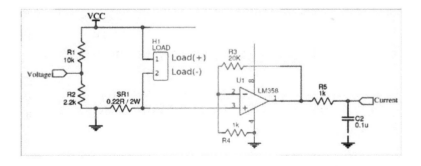

Here the estimation of shunt resistor (SR1) is 0.22 Ohms. As said before we are structuring the circuit for 0-1A so dependent on Ohms law we can ascertain the voltage drop over this resistor which will be around

0.2V when a limit of 1A current is going through the heap. This voltage is little for a microcontroller to peruse, we utilize an Op-Amp in Non-Inverting Amplifier mode to build the voltage from 0.2V to higher level for the Arduino to peruse.

The Op-Amp in Non-Inverting mode is appeared previously. The speaker is intended to have an increase of 21, so 0.2*21 = 4.2V. The formulae to ascertain the increase of the Op-amp is given underneath, you can likewise utilize this online addition number cruncher to get the estimation of your resistor on the off chance that you are re-planning the circuit.

Gain = Vout / Vin = 1 + (Rf / Rin)

Here for our situation the estimation of Rf is 20k and the estimation of Rin is 1k which gives us a gian estimation of 21. The enhanced voltage structure the Op-amp is then given to a RC channel with resistor 1k and a capacitor 0.1uF to channel any commotion that is coupled. At last the voltage is then nourished to the Arduino simple stick.

The last part that is left in the estimating unit is the voltage controller part. Since we will give a variable information voltage we need a managed +5V volt for the Arduino and the Op-amp to work. This controlled voltage will be given by the 7805 Voltage controller. A capacitor is added at the yield to channel the clamor.

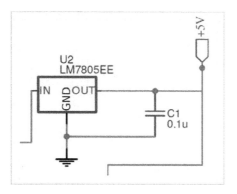

Computation and display unit

In the estimating unit we have planned the circuit to change over the Voltage and Current parameters into 0-5V which can be nourished to the Arduino Analog pins. Presently in this piece of the circuit we will associate these voltage sign to Arduino and furthermore interface a 16×2 alphanumeric presentation to the Arduino with the goal that we can see the outcomes. The circuit for the equivalent is demonstrated as follows

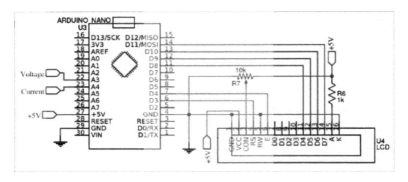

As should be obvious the Voltage stick is associated with Analog stick A3 and the present stick is associated with Analog stick A4. The LCD is controlled from the +5V from the 7805 and is associated with the advanced pins of Arduino to work in 4-piece mode. We have likewise utilized a potentiometer (10k) associated with Con stick to differ the difference of the LCD.

Programming the Arduino

Since we have a decent comprehension of the equipment, let us open the Arduino and start programming. The motivation behind the code is to peruse the simple voltage on stick A3 and A4 and compute the Voltage, Current and Power worth lastly show it on the LCD screen. The total program to do the equivalent is given toward the part of the bargain which can be utilized all things considered for the equipment examined previously. Further the code is part into little scraps and clarified.

As all projects we start with, characterizing the pins

that we have utilized. In out task the A3 and A4 stick is utilized to quantify voltage and current individually and the advanced pins 3,4,8,9,10 and 11 is utilized for interfacing the LCD with Arduino

```
int Read_Voltage = A3;

int Read_Current = A4;

const int rs = 3, en = 4, d4 = 8, d5 = 9, d6 = 10, d7 =
11; //Mention the pin number for LCD connection

LiquidCrystal lcd(rs, en, d4, d5, d6, d7);
```

We additionally have incorporated a header document considered fluid precious stone to interface the LCD with Arduino. At that point inside the arrangement work we initialise the LCD show and show an introduction message as "Arduino Wattmeter" and hang tight for two seconds before clearing it. The code for the equivalent is demonstrated as follows.

```
void setup() {

  lcd.begin(16, 2); //Initialise 16*2 LCD

  lcd.print(" Arduino Wattmeter"); //Intro Message line 1
```

```
lcd.setCursor(0, 1);

lcd.print("-Hello"); //Intro Message line 2

delay(2000);

lcd.clear();

}
```

Inside the primary circle work, we utilize the simple read capacity to peruse the voltage esteem from the stick A3 and A4. As we probably am aware the Arduino ADC yield an incentive from 0-1203 since it has a 10-piece ADC. This worth must be then changed over to 0-5V which should be possible by duplicating with (5/1023). At the same time prior in the equipment we have mapped the real estimation of voltage from 0-24V to 0-5V and the genuine estimation of current structure 0-1A to 0-5V. So now we need to utilize a multiplier to return these qualities to genuine worth. This should be possible by increasing it with a multiplier esteem. The estimation of the multiplier can either be determined hypothetically utilizing the formulae gave in equipment area or in case you have a known arrangement of voltage and current qualities you can ascertain it for all ways as well as purposes. I have pursued the last choice since it will in general be increasingly precise progressively. So here the estimation of multipliers is

6.46 and 0.239. Henceforth the code looks like underneath

```
float Voltage_Value = analogRead(Read_Voltage);

float Current_Value = analogRead(Read_Current);

Voltage_Value = Voltage_Value * (5.0/1023.0) * 6.46;

Current_Value = Current_Value * (5.0/1023.0) * 0.239;
```

How to measure with more accuracy?

The above method for computing the estimation of Actual Voltage and current will work fine and dandy. Be that as it may, experiences one disadvantage, that is the connection between the deliberate ADC voltage and genuine voltage won't be direct thus a solitary multiplier won't give exceptionally exact outcomes, a similar connected for current too.

So to improve the precision we can plot of set of estimated ADC values with real vales utilizing a known arrangement of qualities and afterward utilize that information to plot a chart and determine the multiplier condition utilizing the direct relapse strategy. You can allude the Arduino dB meter in which I have utilized a comparable strategy.

At last, when we have determined the estimation of real voltage and real current through the heap, we can figure the Power utilizing the formulae (P = V*I). At that point we show all the three qualities on the LCD show utilizing the code underneath.

```
lcd.setCursor(0, 0);

lcd.print("V="); lcd.print(Voltage_Value);

lcd.print(" ");

lcd.print("I=");lcd.print(Current_Value);

float Power_Value = Voltage_Value * Current_Value;

lcd.setCursor(0, 1);

lcd.print("Power="); lcd.print(Power_Value);
```

Working and Testing

For instructional exercise I have utilized a perf board to bind every one of the parts as appeared in the circuit. I have utilized a Phoenix screw terminal to interface the heap and ordinary DC barrel Jack to associate my capacity source. The Arduino Nano board and the LCD are mounted on a Female Bergstik with the goal that they can be re-utilized whenever required later.

In the wake of preparing the equipment, transfer the Arduino code to your Nano board. Modify the trimmer pot to control the complexity level of the LCD until you see an unmistakable introduction content. To test the board associate the heap to the screw terminal connector and the source to the Barrel jack. The source voltage ought to be more than 6V for this undertaking to work, since the Arduino required +5V to work. On the off chance that everything is working fine you should see the estimation of Voltage over the heap and the current through it showed in the principal line of the LCD and the determined power showed on the second line of the LCD as demonstrated as follows.

The fun piece of structure something lies in testing it to check how far it will function appropriately. To do that I have utilized 12V vehicle marker buddies as burden and the RPS as source. Since the RPS itself can quantify and show the estimation of current and voltage it will be simple for us to cross check the precision and execution of our circuit. Furthermore, indeed, I likewise utilized my RPS to adjust my multiplier esteem with the goal that I draw near to precise worth.

Expectation you comprehended the circuit and program and got the hang of something helpful.

This Arduino based Wattmeter task has a lot more redesigns that can be added to expand the presentation to auto information logging, plotting chart, telling over voltage or over current circumstances and so on. So remain inquisitive and let me comprehend what you would utilize this for.

Code

```
/*
* Wattmeter for Solar PV using Arduino
*
* Power LCD and circuitry from the +5V pin of Arduino whcih is powered via 7805
* LCD RS -> pin 2
* LCD EN -> pin 3
```

```
* LCD D4 -> pin 8
* LCD D5 -> pin 9
* LCD D6 -> pin 10
* LCD D7 -> pin 11
* Potetnital divider to measure voltage -> A3
* Op-Amp output to measure current -> A4
*/
#include <LiquidCrystal.h>  //Default Arduino LCD
Librarey is included
int Read_Voltage = A3;
int Read_Current = A4;
const int rs = 3, en = 4, d4 = 8, d5 = 9, d6 = 10, d7 = 11; //
Mention the pin number for LCD connection
LiquidCrystal lcd(rs, en, d4, d5, d6, d7);
void setup() {
 lcd.begin(16, 2); //Initialise 16*2 LCD
  lcd.print(" Arduino Wattmeter"); //Intro Message
line 1
 lcd.setCursor(0, 1);
 lcd.print(" With Arduino "); //Intro Message line 2
  delay(2000);
 lcd.clear();
}
void loop() {


 float Voltage_Value = analogRead(Read_Voltage);
 float Current_Value = analogRead(Read_Current);
 Voltage_Value = Voltage_Value * (5.0/1023.0) * 6.46;
 Current_Value = Current_Value * (5.0/1023.0) * 0.239;
```

```
lcd.setCursor(0, 0);
lcd.print("V="); lcd.print(Voltage_Value);
lcd.print(" ");
lcd.print("I=");lcd.print(Current_Value);
float Power_Value = Voltage_Value * Current_Value;
lcd.setCursor(0, 1);
lcd.print("Power="); lcd.print(Power_Value);


delay(200);
}
```

8.DIY SELF BALANCING ROBOT USING ARDUINO

Subsequent to being roused by RYNO engines and other self-adjusting bikes from Segway, I constantly needed to manufacture something comparative. Along these lines I would almost certainly get a handle on the basic idea driving every one of these bikes and furthermore figure out how PID calculation functions.

When I began building, I understood that this bot is somewhat of a test to manufacture. There are such a significant number of choices to choose from and henceforth the perplexities start right structure choosing the engines and stays till tuning PID esteems. What's more, there are such huge numbers of interesting points like sort of battery, position of battery, wheel grasp, kind of engine driver, keeping up the CoG (Center of gravity) and considerably more.

Be that as it may, let me break it to you, when you construct it you will concur that it's not as hard as it sounds to be. So let's be honest, in this instructional exercise I will archive my involvement in structure oneself adjusting robot. You may be a flat out learner who is simply beginning or may have arrived up here after a long disappointment of not getting your bot to work. This spot intends to be your last goal. So we should get started......

Selecting the Parts for your Bot

Before I reveal to all of you the choices for structure the bot let me list the things that I have utilized in this venture

- L298N Motor Driver Module
- Arduino UNO
- Geared DC motors (Yellow colored) – 2Nos
- MPU6050

- A pair of wheels
- Connecting wires
- 7.4V Li-ion Battery
- 3D Printed Body

Controller: The controller that I have utilized is Arduino UNO, why since it is basically simple to utilize. You can likewise utilize an Arduino Nano or Arduino smaller than expected however I would prescribe you to stay with UNO since we can program it legitimately with no outer equipment.

Engines: The best decision of engine that you can use for a self-adjusting robot, unquestionably will be Stepper engine. In any case, To keep things basic I have utilized a DC rigging engine. Truly it isn't compulsory to have a stepper; the bot works fine with these shoddy normally accessible yellow hued DC apparatus engines also.

Engine Driver: If you have chosen the DC apparatus engines like mine then you can either utilize the L298N driver module like me, or even a L293D should work fine and dandy. Become familiar with controlling DC engine utilizing L293D and Arduino.

Wheels: Do not under gauge these folks; I had an intense time making sense of that the issue was with my wheels. So ensure your wheels have great holThe accompanying table will list how the MPU6050 and L298N engine driver module is associated with Arduinod over the floor you are utilizing. Watch intently, your grasp ought to never enable your wheels to production on the floor.

Accelerometer and Gyroscope: The best decision of Accelerometer and Gyroscope for your bot will be the MPU6050. So don't endeavor to assemble one with an ordinary Accelerometer like ADXL345 or something to that effect, it just won't work. You will know why toward the part of the arrangement. You can likewise check our devoted article on utilizing MPU6050 with Arduino.

Battery: We need a battery that is as light as could be expected under the circumstances and the working voltage ought to be beyond what 5V so we can control our Arduino legitimately without a lift module. So the perfect decision will be a 7.4V Li-polymer battery. Here, since I had a 7.4V Li-particle battery promptly accessible I have utilized it. In any case, recall a Li-po is profitable than Li-particle.

Skeleton: Another spot where you ought not bargain is with your bots case. You can utilize cardboard, wood, plastic anything that you are great with. Yet, simply ensure the frame is strong and ought not squirm when the bot is attempting to adjust. I have planned by claim frame on Solid works construing from different bots and 3D printed it. On the off chance that you have a printer, at that point you can likewise print the structure, the plan records will be appended in the up and coming heading.

3D Printing and Assembling the Bot

On the off chance that you have chosen to 3D print a similar case that I am utilizing to fabricate my bot, at that point the STL records can be downloaded from thing verse. I have likewise included the plan records alongside it so you can likewise alter it according to your work force inclinations.

The parts have no overhanging structures so you can undoubtedly print them with no backings and an in-fill of 25% will work fine. The plans are entirely plain and any essential printer ought to have the option to deal with it easily. I utilized the Cura programming to cut the model and printed utilizing my Tevo Tarantula, the setting are demonstrated as follows.

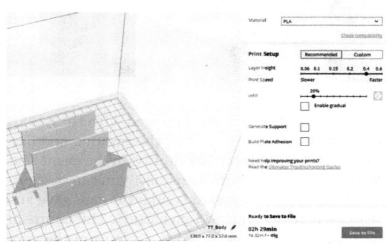

You would need to print the body part just as four

engine mounting parts. The amassing is quite straight forward; utilize 3mm stray pieces to verify the engine and sheets set up. Subsequent to amassing it should look something like this appeared in the image beneath.

The genuine structure was arranged with the L298N drive module in the base rack the Arduino and battery over it as appeared previously. In the event that you are following a similar request you can straightforwardly screw the board trough the gaps gave and utilize a wire tag for the Li-po battery. This course of action ought to likewise work, aside from the very plain wheels which I needed to change later.

In my bot I have swapped the situation of battery and Arduino UNO board for simplicity of programming and furthermore needed to present a perf board for finishing the associations. So my bot did not look as I arranged in starting stage. Subsequent to finishing the wiring programming testing and everything, my bot at last resembles this

Circuit Diagram

Making the associations for this Arduino based Self adjusting Robot is entirely straightforward. We simply need to interface the MPU6050 with Arduino and associate the engines however the Motor driver module. The whole set-up is controlled by the 7.4V li-particle battery. The circuit outline for the equivalent is demonstrated as follows.

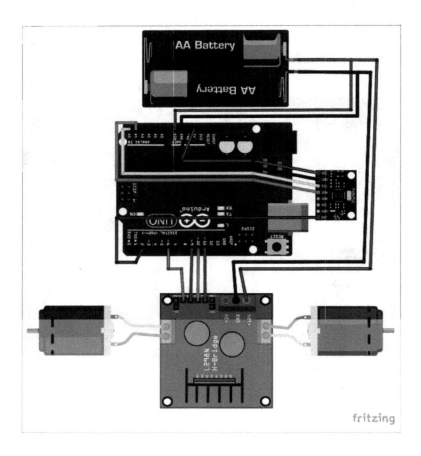

The arduino as well as the l298n engine driver module is direct fueled through the Vin stick as well as the 12V terminal independently. The on-board controller on the Arduino board will modify over the data 7.4V to 5V as well as the ATmega IC as well as MPU6050 will be fueled by it. The DC engines can keep running from voltage 5V to 12V. In any case, we will interface the 7.4V positive wire from battery to 12V info terminal of engine driver module. This will cause the engines to work with 7.4V. The going with table will list how the MPU6050 as well as L298N motor driver module is related with Arduino .

Component Pin	Arduino Pin
MPU6050	
Vcc	+5V
Ground	Gnd
SCL	A5
SDA	A4
INT	D2
L298N	
IN1	D6
IN2	D9
IN3	D10
IN4	D11

The MPU6050 speaks with Arduino through I2C interface, so we utilize the SPI pins A4 as well as A5 of Arduino. The DC engines are associated with PWM pins D6,D9 D10 as well as D11 individually. We have to interface them to PWM pins since we will control the speed of the DC engine by fluctuating the obligation cycle of the PWM signals. In case you are inexperienced with these two segments, at that point it is prescribed to peruse MPU6050 Interfacing and L298N Motor driver instructional exercise.

Programming the Self Balancing Robot

Presently we need to program our Arduino UNO board to adjust the robot. This is the place all the enchantment occurs; the idea driving it is straightforward. We need to check if the bot is inclining towards the front or towards the back utilizing the MPU6050 and after that if it's inclining towards the front we need to pivot the wheels forward path as well as in case it is slanting towards the back we have to turn the wheels in the rearrange course.

Simultaneously we likewise need to control the speed at which wheels are turning, if the bot is somewhat perplexed from focus position the wheels pivot gradually and the speed increment as it makes tracks in an opposite direction from the inside position. To accomplish this rationale we utilize the PID calculation, which has the middle position as set-point and the degree of confusion as the yield.

To know the current position of the bot we use the MPU6050, which is a 6-hub accelerometer and whirligig sensor joined. In order to get a strong estimation of position from the sensor we need to use the estimation of both accelerometer just as whirligig, in light in case the Characteristics from accelerometer has disturbance issues and the characteristics from gyrator will in general float with time. So we have to join both as well as get the estimation of yaw pitch as well as move of our robot of which we will utilize just the estimation of yaw.

Sounds bit of head reeling right? In any case, stress not, on account of the Arduino people group we have promptly accessible libraries that can play out the PID count and furthermore get the estimation of yaw from the MPU6050. The library is created by br3ttb and jrowberg separately. Before continuing download their libraries structure the accompanying connection and add them to your Arduino lib registry.

https://github.com/br3ttb/Arduino-PID-Library/mass/ace/PID_v1.h

https://github.com/jrowberg/i2cdevlib/tree/ace/Arduino/MPU6050

Currently, we has the libraries added to our Arduino IDE. How about we start programming for our Self adjusting Robot. Like consistently the total code for the Project is given toward the part of the arrangement, here I am simply clarifying the most significant bits in the code. A told before the code is expand over the MPU6050 model code we are simply going to improve the code for our motivation and include the PID and control procedure for our self adjusting robot.

First we incorporate the libraries that are required for this program to work. They incorporate the inmanufactured I2C library, PID Library and MPU6050 Library that we just downloaded.

```
#include "I2Cdev.h"

#include    <PID_v1.h>    //From    https://
github.com/br3ttb/Arduino-PID-Library/blob/
master/PID_v1.h

#include         "MPU6050_6Axis_MotionApp-
s20.h"   //https://github.com/jrowberg/i2cdev-
lib/tree/master/Arduino/MPU6050
```

At that point we announce the factors that are required to get the information from the MPU6050 sensor. We read both the gravity vector and quaternion esteems and after that figure the yaw pitch and move estimation of the bot. The buoy exhibit ypr[3] will hold the last outcome.

```
// MPU control/status vars

bool dmpReady = false; // set true if DMP init was
successful

uint8_t mpuIntStatus;   // holds actual interrupt
status byte from MPU

uint8_t devStatus;   // return status after each de-
vice operation (0 = success, !0 = error)

uint16_t packetSize;  // expected DMP packet size
(default is 42 bytes)

uint16_t fifoCount;     // count of all bytes cur-
rently in FIFO

uint8_t fifoBuffer[64]; // FIFO storage buffer

// orientation/motion vars

Quaternion q;        // [w, x, y, z]        quaternion
container

VectorFloat gravity; // [x, y, z]      gravity vector

float ypr[3];      // [yaw, pitch, roll] yaw/pitch/roll
container and gravity vector
```

Next comes the significant section of the code, and this is the place you will spend quite a while in tuning for the correct arrangement of qualities. On the off chance that you robot is worked with a generally excellent focus of gravity and the segments are evenly orchestrated (which by and large isn't) at that point the estimation of your set-point will be 180. Else interface your bot to Arduino sequential screen and tilt it till you locate a decent adjusting position, read the worth showed on sequential screen and this is your set point esteem. The estimation of Kp, Kd as well as Ki must be tuned by your bot. No two indistinguishable bots will have similar estimations of Kp, Kd and Ki so there is no getting away from it.

/*********Tune these 4 values for your BOT*********/

double setpoint= 176; //set the value when the bot is perpendicular to ground using serial monitor.

double Kp = 21; //Set this first

double Kd = 0.8; //Set this secound

double Ki = 140; //Finally set this

/******End of values setting*********/

In the following line we initialise the PID calculation by passing the information factors input, yield, set point, Kp, Ki as well as Kd. We have effectively set the estimations of set-point Kp,Ki as well as Kd in the above bit of code. The estimation of info will be the present estimation of yaw that is perused from the MPU6050 sensor and the estimation of yield will be the worth that is determined by the PID calculation. So fundamentally the PID calculation will give us a yield esteem which ought to be utilized to address the Input an incentive to being it near the set point.

> **PID pid(&input, &output, &setpoint, Kp, Ki, Kd, DIRECT);**

Inside the void arrangement work we begin the MPU6050 by designing the DMP (Digital Motion Processor). This will help us in joining the Accelerometer information with Gyroscope information and give a solid estimation of Yaw, Pitch and Roll. We won't dive much deep into this since it will be a long ways past the theme. In any case one fragment of code that you need to turn upward in the arrangement capacity is the gyro counterbalanced qualities. Each MPU6050 sensor has its own estimations of counterbalances you can utilize this Arduino sketch to ascertain the balance estimation of you sensor and update the accompanying lines in like manner in your program.

> **// supply your own gyro offsets here, scaled for min sensitivity**

```
mpu.setXGyroOffset(220);

mpu.setYGyroOffset(76);

mpu.setZGyroOffset(-85);

mpu.setZAccelOffset(1688);
```

We likewise need to initialise the Digital PWM pins that we are utilizing to interface our engines to. For our situation it is D6, D9, D10 and D11. So we initialise these pins as yield pins make them LOW of course.

```
//Initialise the Motor outpu pins

    pinMode (6, OUTPUT);

    pinMode (9, OUTPUT);

    pinMode (10, OUTPUT);

    pinMode (11, OUTPUT);

  //By default turn off both the motors

    analogWrite(6,LOW);

    analogWrite(9,LOW);
```

```
analogWrite(10,LOW);

analogWrite(11,LOW);
```

Inside the primary circle work we check if the information from the MPU6050 is prepared to be perused. In case truly, at that point we use it to register the PID worth and afterward show the info and yield estimation of PID on sequential screen just to check how the PID is reacting. At that point dependent on the estimation of yield we choose if the bot needs to push ahead or in reverse or stop.

Since we expect that the MPU6050 will return 180 when the bot is upstanding. We will get redress esteems positive when the bot is falling towards front and we will get values in negative if the bot is falling towards back. So we check for this condition and call the fitting capacities to push the bot ahead or back ward.

```
while (!mpuInterrupt && fifoCount < packetSize)

{

    //no mpu data - performing PID calculations
and output to motors

    pid.Compute();
```

```
    //Print the value of Input and Output on ser-
ial monitor to check how it is working.

    Serial.print(input); Serial.print(" =>"); Ser-
ial.println(output);

    if (input>150 && input<200){//If the Bot is
falling

    if (output>0) //Falling towards front

    Forward(); //Rotate the wheels forward

    else if (output<0) //Falling towards back

    Reverse(); //Rotate the wheels backward

    }

    else //If Bot not falling

    Stop(); //Hold the wheels still

}
```

The PID yield variable likewise chooses how quick
the engine must be turned. On the off chance that
the bot is going to fall, at that point we make minor
redress by turning the wheel gradually. In the event
that these minor adjustment dint work and still if the

bot is tumbling down we increment the speed of the engine. The estimation of how quick the wheels turn will be chosen by the PI calculation. Note that for the Reverse capacity we have duplicated the estimation of yield with - 1 so we can change over the negative an incentive to positive.

```
void Forward() //Code to rotate the wheel forward

{

    analogWrite(6,output);

    analogWrite(9,0);

    analogWrite(10,output);

    analogWrite(11,0);

    Serial.print("F"); //Debugging information

}

void Reverse() //Code to rotate the wheel Backward

{

    analogWrite(6,0);
```

```
    analogWrite(9,output*-1);

    analogWrite(10,0);

    analogWrite(11,output*-1);

  Serial.print("R");

}

void Stop() //Code to stop both the wheels

{

    analogWrite(6,0);

    analogWrite(9,0);

    analogWrite(10,0);

    analogWrite(11,0);

    Serial.print("S");

}
```

Working of Arduino Self Balancing Robot

When you are prepared with the equipment, you can transfer the code to your Arduino board. Ensure the associations are legitimate since we are utilizing a Li-particle battery extraordinary alert is required. So twofold check for shortcircuits and guarantee that the terminals won't come into contact regardless of whether your bot encounters some little impacts. Catalyst your module and open your sequential screen, if your Arduino could speak with MPU6050 effectively and if everything is functioning true to form you should see the accompanying screen.

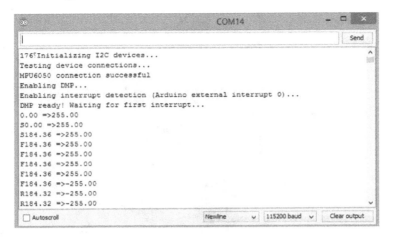

Here we see the information and yield estimations of the PID calculation in the configuration input => yield. In the event that the bot is splendidly balance the estimation of yield will be 0. The information worth is the present an incentive from the MPU6050 sensor. The letters in order "F" speaks to that the bot is moving in forward and "R" speaks to that the bot in turn around.

During the underlying phases of PID I prescribe leaving your Arduino link associated with the bot so you can without much of a stretch screen the estimations of info and yield and furthermore it will be anything but difficult to address and transfer your program for Kp, Ki and Kd values.

Expectation this assembles your own self adjusting robot.

Code

```
/*Arduino Self Balancing Robot
 * Build on top of Lib: https://github.com/jrowberg/
i2cdevlib/tree/master/Arduino/MPU6050

 */
#include "I2Cdev.h"
#include <PID_v1.h> //From  https://github.com/
br3ttb/Arduino-PID-Library/blob/master/PID_v1.h
#include              "MPU6050_6Axis_MotionApp-
s20.h"    //https://github.com/jrowberg/i2cdevlib/
tree/master/Arduino/MPU6050
MPU6050 mpu;
// MPU control/status vars
bool dmpReady = false; // set true if DMP init was suc-
cessful
uint8_t mpuIntStatus;   // holds actual interrupt sta-
tus byte from MPU
uint8_t devStatus;    // return status after each device
operation (0 = success, !0 = error)
uint16_t packetSize;    // expected DMP packet size
(default is 42 bytes)
uint16_t fifoCount;    // count of all bytes currently in
FIFO
uint8_t fifoBuffer[64]; // FIFO storage buffer
// orientation/motion vars
Quaternion q;       // [w, x, y, z]    quaternion container
VectorFloat gravity;  // [x, y, z]       gravity vector
float ypr[3];         // [yaw, pitch, roll]  yaw/pitch/roll
```

container and gravity vector

```
/*********Tune these 4 values for your BOT********/
double setpoint= 176; //set the value when the bot is
perpendicular to ground using serial monitor.
double Kp = 21; //Set this first
double Kd = 0.8; //Set this secound
double Ki = 140; //Finally set this
/******End of values setting********/
double input, output;
PID pid(&input, &output, &setpoint, Kp, Ki, Kd, DIR-
ECT);
volatile bool mpuInterrupt = false;      // indicates
whether MPU interrupt pin has gone high
void dmpDataReady()
{
  mpuInterrupt = true;
}
void setup() {
 Serial.begin(115200);
  //initialize device
  Serial.println(F("Initializing I2C devices..."));
  mpu.initialize();
    //verify connection
  Serial.println(F("Testing device connections..."));
   Serial.println(mpu.testConnection() ? F("MPU6050
connection successful") : F("MPU6050 connection
failed"));
    //load and configure the DMP
  devStatus = mpu.dmpInitialize();
```

```
    // supply your own gyro offsets here, scaled for
min sensitivity
  mpu.setXGyroOffset(220);
  mpu.setYGyroOffset(76);
  mpu.setZGyroOffset(-85);
  mpu.setZAccelOffset(1688);
    // make sure it worked (returns 0 if so)
  if (devStatus == 0)
  {
  // turn on the DMP, now that it's ready
  Serial.println(F("Enabling DMP..."));
  mpu.setDMPEnabled(true);

  // enable Arduino interrupt detection
  Serial.println(F("Enabling interrupt detection (Ar-
duino external interrupt 0)..."));
  attachInterrupt(0, dmpDataReady, RISING);
  mpuIntStatus = mpu.getIntStatus();

    // set our DMP Ready flag so the main loop()
function knows it's okay to use it
  Serial.println(F("DMP ready! Waiting for first inter-
rupt..."));
  dmpReady = true;

    // get expected DMP packet size for later com-
parison
  packetSize = mpu.dmpGetFIFOPacketSize();


    //setup PID
```

```
    pid.SetMode(AUTOMATIC);
    pid.SetSampleTime(10);
    pid.SetOutputLimits(-255, 255);
  }
  else
  {
    // ERROR!
    // 1 = initial memory load failed
    // 2 = DMP configuration updates failed
    // (if it's going to break, usually the code will be 1)
    Serial.print(F("DMP Initialization failed (code "));
    Serial.print(devStatus);
    Serial.println(F(")"));
  }
//Initialise the Motor outpu pins
  pinMode (6, OUTPUT);
  pinMode (9, OUTPUT);
  pinMode (10, OUTPUT);
  pinMode (11, OUTPUT);
//By default turn off both the motors
  analogWrite(6,LOW);
  analogWrite(9,LOW);
  analogWrite(10,LOW);
  analogWrite(11,LOW);
}
void loop() {


    // if programming failed, don't try to do anything
    if (!dmpReady) return;
```

```
// wait for MPU interrupt or extra packet(s) avail-
able
  while (!mpuInterrupt && fifoCount < packetSize)
  {
    //no mpu data - performing PID calculations and
output to motors
    pid.Compute();


    //Print the value of Input and Output on serial
monitor to check how it is working.
        Serial.print(input); Serial.print(" =>"); Ser-
ial.println(output);


        if(input>150 && input<200){//If the Bot is fall-
ing


    if(output>0) //Falling towards front
    Forward(); //Rotate the wheels forward
    else if(output<0) //Falling towards back
    Reverse(); //Rotate the wheels backward
    }
    else //If Bot not falling
    Stop(); //Hold the wheels still


    }
    // reset interrupt flag and get INT_STATUS byte
    mpuInterrupt = false;
    mpuIntStatus = mpu.getIntStatus();
```

```
// get current FIFO count
fifoCount = mpu.getFIFOCount();
// check for overflow (this should never happen
unless our code is too inefficient)
if((mpuIntStatus & 0x10) || fifoCount == 1024)
{
// reset so we can continue cleanly
mpu.resetFIFO();
Serial.println(F("FIFO overflow!"));
// otherwise, check for DMP data ready interrupt
(this should happen frequently)
}
else if(mpuIntStatus & 0x02)
{
// wait for correct available data length, should be
a VERY short wait
    while (fifoCount < packetSize) fifoCount =
mpu.getFIFOCount();
// read a packet from FIFO
mpu.getFIFOBytes(fifoBuffer, packetSize);


// track FIFO count here in case there is > 1
packet available
// (this lets us immediately read more without
waiting for an interrupt)
fifoCount -= packetSize;
    mpu.dmpGetQuaternion(&q, fifoBuffer); //get
value for q
mpu.dmpGetGravity(&gravity, &q); //get value for
```

gravity

    mpu.dmpGetYawPitchRoll(ypr, &q, &gravity); // get value for ypr

```
    input = ypr[1]* 180/M_PI + 180;
  }
}
void Forward() //Code to rotate the wheel forward
{
  analogWrite(6,output);
  analogWrite(9,0);
  analogWrite(10,output);
  analogWrite(11,0);
  Serial.print("F"); //Debugging information
}
void Reverse() //Code to rotate the wheel Backward
{
  analogWrite(6,0);
  analogWrite(9,output*-1);
  analogWrite(10,0);
  analogWrite(11,output*-1);
  Serial.print("R");
}
void Stop() //Code to stop both the wheels
{
  analogWrite(6,0);
  analogWrite(9,0);
  analogWrite(10,0);
  analogWrite(11,0);
  Serial.print("S");
}
```

9.CONTROLLING ARDUINO WITH RASPBERRY PI USING PYFIRMATA

In spite of the fact that Raspberry Pi and Arduino are two diverse equipment regarding their applications and structure, yet the two of them are considered as two contending open source equipment stages. The two of them have extremely solid network and backing. Today we will somewhat change things, and demonstrate to you how we can exploit them two. In the event that you have both Arduino and Raspberry pi sheets, this article will tell you the best way to utilize Raspberry pi and Python to control the Arduino.

We will utilize PyFirmata firmware to offer directions to Arduino utilizing Raspberry Pi python content. PyFirmata is essentially a prebuilt library bundle of python program which can be introduced in Arduino to permit sequential correspondence between a python content on any PC and an Arduino. This python bundle can offer access to peruse and compose any stick on the Arduino. So here we will run python program on Arduino utilizing Raspberry pi.

So in this instructional exercise we will exploit this library and will utilize this in our Arduino board to control Arduino utilizing Raspberry Pi.
Requirements

1. Arduino Uno or some other Arduino board

2. Raspberry Pi with Raspbian OS introduced in it

3. LED

4. Arduino USB cable

In this instructional exercise I am utilizing External Monitor utilizing HDMI link to associate with Raspberry Pi. On the off chance that you don't have screen, you can utilize SSH customer (Putty) or VNC server to associate with Raspberry pi utilizing Laptop or PC. In case you discover any trouble, at that point pursue our Getting gazed with Raspberry Pi Guide.

Installing PyFirmata in Arduino using Raspberry Pi

To transfer PyFirmata firmware in Arduino, we need to introduce Arduino IDE in Raspberry Pi. Pursue these means to introduce:

Stage 1:- Connect the Raspberry Pi to the web. Open direction terminal and type the accompanying order and hit enter

```
sudo apt-get -y install arduino python-serial mercurial
```

Hang tight for couple of minutes, it will require some serious energy. This direction will introduce the Arduino IDE in your Raspberry Pi.

Stage 2:- Now, we will introduce pyFirmata documents utilizing the given github:

```
git clone https://github.com/tino/pyFirmata
```

At that point run the accompanying order:

```
cd pyFirmata

sudo python setup.py install
```

Stage 3:- We have introduced all the required documents and arrangements.

Presently, interface your Arduino board with Raspberry Pi utilizing USB link and dispatch Arduino IDE by composing arduino in terminal window.

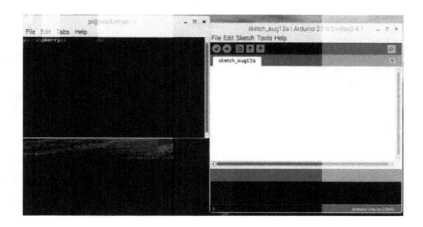

Stage 4:- Then type lsusb direction to check whether Arduino is associated with your raspberry pi.

In Arduino IDE, Go to instruments and pick your board and Serial Port.

Stage 5:- Upload the PyFirmata firmware on the Arduino by clicking File - > Examples - > Firmata - > Standard Firmata and after that snap transfer catch . As demonstrated as follows.

We have effectively introduced the pyFirmata firmware in the Arduino board. Presently, we can control our Arduino utilizing Raspberry Pi.

For exhibition we will flicker and blur a LED on the Arduino by composing python codes in Raspberry Pi.

Code Explanation

For coding part, you should peruse documentation of pyFirmata for better understanding. We will utilize pyFirmata capacities to compose our code. You can discover pyFirmata documentation by following the connection.

So we should begin composing the code

Open your preferred content tool on the Raspberry Pi

and import pyFirmata library.

```
import pyfirmata
```

Characterize stick on the Arduino to interface the LED

```
led_pin = 9
```

Presently, we need to compose sequential port name on which Arduino board is associated utilizing pyfirmata.Arduino() capacity and afterward make an example by allocating port in board variable.

```
board = pyfirmata.Arduino("/dev/ttyACM0")

print "Code is running"
```

In while circle, make drove stick HIGH and low utilizing board.digital[].write() capacity and give postpone utilizing board.pass_time() work.

```
while True:

    board.digital[led_pin].write(0)
```

```
board.pass_time(1)

board.digital[led_pin].write(1)

board.pass_time(1)
```

Our code is prepared, spare this code by putting .py augmentation to the record name.

Open order terminal as well as type python blink.py to run the code on the Arduino board. Ensure your Arduino board is associated with your Raspberry Pi board utilizing USB link.

Presently, you can see Blinking LED on the Arduino board.

Complete code for squinting LED utilizing pyFirmata is given toward the end.

Fading LED on Arduino using pyFirmata

Presently, we will compose code for blurring the LED to make you increasingly acquainted with the py-Firmata capacities. This code is simple as past one. You have to use two for circles, one for increment brilliance and other for diminishing splendor.

In this code, we have characterized the pins in various manner like drove = board.get_pin('d:9:p') where d implies advanced stick. This is capacity of py-Firmata library. Peruse the documentation for more subtleties.

Complete code for Fading LED utilizing pyFirmata is given toward the end.

Presently, you can add more sensors to your framework and make it increasingly cool, check our other Arduino activities and take a stab at structure them utilizing Raspberry pi and python content.

Code

Python code for LED blink:

```
import pyfirmata
led_pin = 9
board = pyfirmata.Arduino("/dev/ttyACM0")
while True:
  board.digital[led_pin].write(0)
  board.pass_time(1)
  board.digital[led_pin].write(1)
  board.pass_time(1)
```

Python code for Fading LED:

```
import time
import pyfirmata
delay = 0.3
brightness = 0
board = pyfirmata.Arduino("/dev/ttyACM0")
led = board.get_pin('d:9:p')
while True:
# increase
```

```python
for i in range(0, 10):
    brightness = brightness + 0.1
    print "Setting brightness to %s" % brightness
    led.write(brightness)
    board.pass_time(delay)
# decrease
for i in range(0, 10):
    print "Setting brightness to %s" % brightness
    led.write(brightness)
    brightness = brightness - 0.1
    board.pass_time(delay)
```

10.ARDUINO BASED REAL-TIME OSCILLOSCOPE

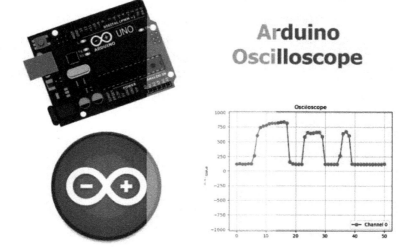

The Oscilloscope is one of the most significant apparatuses you will discover on the workbench of any hardware specialist or creator. It is basically utilized for survey waveform and deciding voltage levels, recurrence, commotion and different parameters of sign connected at its information that may change after some time. It is additionally utilized by inserted programming designers for code investigating and professionals for investigating electronic gadgets during fix. These reasons make the oscilloscope an absolute necessity have apparatus for any designer. The main issue is they can be pricey, Oscilloscopes that plays out the most fundamental of capacities with the least exactness can be as costly as $45 to $100 while the further developed and effective have cost over a $150. Today I will show how to utilize the Arduino and a product, which will be created with my preferred programming language Python, to construct an ease, 4-channel Arduino oscilloscope fit for playing out the errands for which a portion of the modest oscilloscope are sent like the presentation of waveforms and assurance of voltage levels for sign.

How it works

There are two sections for this undertaking;

- The Data Converter

- The Plotter

Oscilloscopes for the most part include the visual portrayal of a simple sign connected to its information channel. To accomplish this, we have to initially change over the sign from simple to advanced and after that plot the information. For the transformation, we will use on the ADC (Analog to Digital converter) on the atmega328p microcontroller utilized by the Arduino to change over the Analog information at the sign contribution to a computerized sign. After transformation, the worth per time is sent through UART from the Arduino to the PC where the plotter programming which will be created utilizing python will change over the approaching stream of information to a waveform by plotting every datum against time.

Required Components

The accompanying parts are required to manufacture this undertaking;

- Arduino Uno (Any of different sheets can be utilized)
- 10k Resistor (1)
- Breadboard
- Jumper wires
- LDR (1)

Required Softwares

- Python Libraries: Pyserial, Matplotlib, Drawnow
- Python
- Arduino IDE

Schematics

The schematic for the Arduino Oscilloscope is straightforward. We should simply interface the sign to be inspected to the predefined Analog stick of the Arduino. In any case, we will utilize the LDR in a straightforward voltage divider arrangement to produce the sign to be inspected, with the end goal that the created waveform will depict the voltage level, in view of the power of light around the LDR.

Associate the segments as appeared in the schematics beneath;

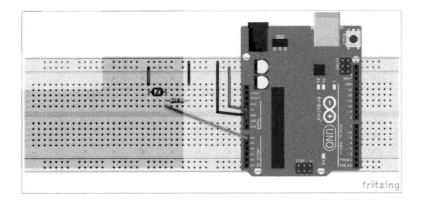

After association, the arrangement should like the picture underneath.

With the associations all done, we can continue to compose the code.

Arduino Osclloscope Code

We will compose codes for every one of the two areas. For the Plotter as referenced before, we will compose a python content that acknowledges the information from the Arduino by means of UART and Plots, while for the converter, we will compose an Arduino sketch that takes in the information from the ADC and changes over it to voltage levels which are sent to the plotter.

Python (Plotter) Script

Since the python code is progressively mind boggling, we will begin with it.

We will utilize a few libraries including; drawnow, Matplotlib and Pyserial with the python content as referenced before. Pyserial enables us to make a python content that can convey over the sequential port, Matplotlib enables us to create plots from the information got over the sequential port and drawnow gives a way to us to refresh the plot progressively.

There are a few different ways to introduce these bundles on your PC, the least demanding being by means of pip. Pip can be introduced by means of direction line on a windows or linux machine. PIP is bundled with python3 so I will prompt you introduce python3 and check the crate about adding python to way. On the off chance that you are having issues with introducing pip, look at this the official python site for tips.

With pip introduced, we would now be able to introduce different libraries we need.

Open the order brief for windows clients, terminal for linux clients and enter the accompanying;

pip install pyserial

With this done, introduce matplotlib utilizing;

pip install matplotlib

Drawnow is in some cases introduced close by matplotlib yet just certainly, run;

pip install drawnow

With the establishment complete, we are currently prepared to compose the python content.

The python content for this task is like the one I composed for the Raspberry Pi Based Oscilloscope.

We start by bringing in every one of the libraries required for the code;

```
import time

import matplotlib.pyplot as plt

from drawnow import *

import pyserial
```

Next, we make and introduce the factors that will be utilized during the code. The exhibit val will be utilized to store the information got from the sequential port and cnt will be utilized to check. Information at area 0 will be erased after each 50 information tallies. This is done to keep the information being shown on the oscilloscope.

```
val = [ ]

cnt = 0
```

Next, we make the sequential port article through which the Arduino will speak with our python content. Guarantee the com port determined beneath is the equivalent com port through which your Arduino board speaks with the IDE. The 115200 baud rate utilized above was utilized to guarantee rapid correspondence with the Arduino. To anticipate blunders, the Arduino sequential port should likewise be empowered to speak with this baud rate.

```
port = serial.Serial('COM4', 115200, timeout=0.5)
```

Next, we make the plot intuitive utilizing;

```
plt.ion()
```

we have to make a capacity to produce the plot from

the information got, making the upper and least limit we are expecting, which for this situation is 1023 dependent on the goals of the Arduino's ADC. We additionally set the title, mark every pivot and add a legend to make it simple to recognize the plot.

```
#create the figure function

def makeFig():

    plt.ylim(-1023,1023)

    plt.title('Osciloscope')

    plt.grid(True)

    plt.ylabel('ADC outputs')

    plt.plot(val, 'ro-', label='Channel 0')

    plt.legend(loc='lower right')
```

With this done, we are currently prepared to compose the primary circle that takes the information from the sequential port when accessible and plots it. To synchronize with the Arduino, a handshake information is sent to the Arduino by the python content to demonstrate its preparation to peruse information. At the point when the Arduino gets the handshake information, it answers with information from the ADC. Without this handshake, we won't most likely plot the information continuously.

```python
while (True):

    port.write(b's') #handshake with Arduino

    if (port.inWaiting()):# if the arduino replies

        value = port.readline()# read the reply

        print(value)#print so we can monitor it

        number = int(value) #convert received data to integer

        print('Channel 0: {0}'.format(number))

        # Sleep for half a second.

        time.sleep(0.01)

        val.append(int(number))

        drawnow(makeFig)#update plot to reflect new data input

        plt.pause(.000001)
```

```
cnt = cnt + 1

if(cnt > 50):

    val.pop(0)#keep the plot fresh by deleting the
data at position 0
```

The total python code for arduino oscilloscope is given toward the part of the arrangement demonstrated as follows.

Arduino code

The subsequent code is the Arduino sketch to acquire the information speaking to the sign from the ADC, at that point hold on to get the handshake signal from the plotter programming. When it gets the handshake signal, it sends the procured information to the plotter programming through UART.

We start by proclaiming the stick of the Analog stick of the Arduino to which the sign will be connected.

```
int sensorpin = A0;
```

Next, we introduce and start sequential correspondence with a baud pace of 115200

```
void setup() {
```

```
    // initialize serial communication at 115200 bits
    per second to match that of the python script:

    Serial.begin(115200);

}
```

In conclusion, the voidloop() work which handles the perusing of the information, and sends the information over sequential to the plotter.

```
void loop() {

    // read the input on analog pin 0:

    float sensorValue = analogRead(sensorpin);

    byte data = Serial.read();

    if (data == 's')

    {

      Serial.println(sensorValue);

      delay(10);    // delay in between reads for stability

    }
```

```
}
```

The total Arduino Oscilloscope Code is given beneath just as toward the part of the arrangement demonstrated as follows.

```
int sensorpin = A0;

void setup() {

   // initialize serial communication at 115200 bits
per second to match that of the python script:

   Serial.begin(115200);

}

void loop() {

   // read the input on analog pin
0:#####################################
###################

   float sensorValue = analogRead(sensorpin);

   byte data = Serial.read();

   if (data == 's')
```

```
{

    Serial.println(sensorValue);

    delay(10);    // delay in between reads for stabil-
ity

}

}
```

Arduino Oscilloscope in Action

Transfer the code to the Arduino arrangement and run the python content. You should see the information start gushing in through the python order line and the plot shifting with the light power as appeared in the picture beneath.

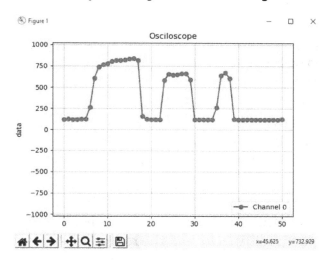

So this is the manner by which Arduino can be utilized as Oscilloscope, it can likewise be made utilizing Raspberry pi, check here the total instructional exercise on Raspberry Pi based Oscilloscope.

Code

Python Code:

```
import time
import matplotlib.pyplot as plt
from drawnow import *
import serial
val = [ ]
cnt = 0
#create the serial port object
port = serial.Serial('COM4', 115200, timeout=0.5)
plt.ion()
```

```python
#create the figure function
def makeFig():
  plt.ylim(-1023,1023)
  plt.title('Osciloscope')
  plt.grid(True)
  plt.ylabel('data')
  plt.plot(val, 'ro-', label='Channel 0')
  plt.legend(loc='lower right')
while (True):
  port.write(b's') #handshake with Arduino
  if(port.inWaiting()):# if the arduino replies
    value = port.readline()# read the reply
    print(value)#print so we can monitor it
    number = int(value) #convert received data to in-
teger
    print('Channel 0: {0}'.format(number))
    # Sleep for half a second.
    time.sleep(0.01)
    val.append(int(number))
      drawnow(makeFig)#update plot to reflect new
data input
    plt.pause(.000001)
    cnt = cnt+1
  if(cnt>50):
    val.pop(0)#keep the plot fresh by deleting the data
at position 0
```

Arduino Code:

```arduino
int sensorpin = A0;
void setup() {
  // initialize serial communication at 115200 bits
```

per second to match that of the python script:

```
 Serial.begin(115200);
}
void loop() {
       // read the input on analog pin
0:###########################################
##################
 float sensorValue = analogRead(sensorpin);
 byte data = Serial.read();
 if(data == 's')
 {
  Serial.println(sensorValue);
  delay(10);    // delay in between reads for stability
 }
}
```